INTRODUCTION: Time to Fly

This is the story of the revolution in air travel that took place between 1945 and 1969 and about the aircraft that made it possible. In that quarter century, commercial aviation would evolve from 28-passenger airliners flying at less than 200 miles per hour to 150-passenger jetliners cruising from continent to continent at 600 miles per hour. This is the story of the last generation of piston-engined flight—the ultimate propliners—and the first generation of jetliners.

The quarter century that began with World War II contained many monumental years for aviation. Not only did aeronautical technology leap further and faster than at any other time in history—before or since—but the whole cultural conception of air travel changed to an equal or greater degree.

During those years, air travel would change from being a novelty to being routine for business travelers and vacationers alike. This was especially true in the United States, where a desire to cover substantial distances with speed and comfort intersected with an era of unprecedented prosperity. It was time to fly.

When the United States emerged from World War II, the first thoughts were "to get back to normal." But "normal" had changed. The cultural and economic reality in the United States had gone through an incredible metamorphosis. Americans had come out of the war with a much broader vision of the world and with a lot more money in their pockets. Their concept of air travel was also soon to change.

In the American commercial aviation market of the late 1940s, three forces converged to create a windfall for air travel. First, a pent-up demand existed for travel by a population that had suffered through the Great Depression, followed by five years of wartime rationing. Second, there was an unprecedented increase in disposable income that came about in part because people had earned good money during the war, and there had been, until late 1945, a paucity of consumer goods on which to spend it. Third was the rapid developments in aviation technology—from avionics to radar to engines—that had occurred during, and because of, the war.

During the first four decades of the twentieth century, people traveling between New York and Chicago or Philadelphia, or between Los Angeles and San Francisco, simply took the train. With the advent of fast, reliable—and routine—air travel, taking the train was just a memory for most people. Travelers would happily say "good riddance" to the overnight trip from New York to Chicago or from Seattle to San Francisco. By air, these distances could be conquered between lunch and dinner.

By the fifties, air travel had become part of everyday life. People, who a generation before would have taken the train, now took the plane without a second thought. A vacation in Hawaii or a trip to Europe, which had—in recent memory—been once-in-a-lifetime events for a mere handful of people, were suddenly plausible for anyone in the rapidly expanding American middle class. People were ready to go, and the airlines were clamoring for newer and bigger airliners to take them.

People could now fly routinely from coast to coast in the United States without stopping two or more times in the middle. This changed everything from family vacations to Major League Baseball. Moving the Dodgers and the Giants from Brooklyn and New York to Los Angeles and San Francisco—as abhorrent as it was to many—would have been unthinkable before jetliners. The travel time between coasts had been just too much to be accommodated within the Major League schedule on a regular basis. With nonstop, five-hour coast-to-coast flights, the National League was truly nationwide, and the American League spanned the whole country.

This book is about that which has been described as the Golden Age of passenger air travel. It came after the "wind-in-your-hair" era of passenger air travel but before the years of "sardine can" overcrowding. It was that era between the time that airliners became routine and the era when cramped seating began to make air travel an experience to be endured rather than enjoyed.

This was the exciting era when air travel—as we have known it since the 1970s—literally defined itself. It was an era of new horizons and exciting innovations, and passengers still found it *fun* to fly.

CONTENTS

First published in 2001 by MBI Publishing Company, Galtier Plaza, Suite 200, 380 Jackson Street, St. Paul, MN 55101-3885 USA

MBI Publishing Company books are also available at discounts in bulk quantity for industrial or sales-promotional use. For details write to Special Sales Manager at Motorbooks International Wholesalers & Distributors, Galtier Plaza, Suite 200, 380 Jackson Street, St. Paul, MN 55101-3885 USA.

Library of Congress Cataloging-in-Publication Data Available
ISBN 0-7603-0913-2

On the front cover: The Flagship Missouri was the third Douglas DC-7 delivered to American Airlines. After ordering the first 25 DC-7s, American pushed its total buy to 58, more than any other airline.

On the frontispiece: A happy pilot offers a thumbs up from the cockpit of a Swissair Model 440-11 Metropolitan. Also a user of the earlier model 240 Convairliner, Swissair took delivery of a dozen Metropolitans.

On the title page: In an eye-popping publicity effort aimed at making its presence known everywhere, Braniff International Airways painted its entire fleet in bright colors. The abstract artist Alexander Calder designed the brilliant markings, illustrated here by a Douglas DC-8-62.

On the back cover, top: The first Boeing Model 377 Stratocruiser in flight in March 1948. Owned by Pan American World Airways, the ship joined Pan Am's fleet as Clipper Nightingale after being used by Boeing for an extensive series of flight tests. The aircraft is seen here in Boeing colors on a test flight prior to painting and delivery to Pan Am.
bottom: Champagne anyone? The passenger cabin of a Convair 880 circa 1959 was a high-class place. Note that smoking was not only permissible, but cigarettes were provided.

Edited by Mike Haenggi
Designed by Katie Sonmor
Printed in Hong Kong

CLASSIC AMERICAN
AIRLINERS

BILL YENNE

MBI Publishing Company

SETTING THE STAGE FOR MODERN AIR TRAVEL

The birth of modern, routine air travel had begun in the late thirties, but the birthing process was rudely interrupted by the beginning of World War II.

The process began in August 1936 with the delivery to American Airlines of the first Douglas DC-3. This aircraft is one of the undisputed greats of aviation, and it was probably the most important and most successful airliner in service anywhere at any time during the years before World War II. More important, it represented a turning point in the way that people thought about air travel.

Soon after American Airlines began operating its DC-3s, TWA and Eastern Airlines, as well as United Air Lines, placed orders. Within three years, nine out of every ten airliners operated by U.S. airlines was either a DC-3 or its predecessor, the similar, but less capable, DC-2. When World War II started in 1939, and a total of 455 DC-3s had been delivered to airlines around the world.

The DC-3 had quickened the evolution of commercial air travel and brought it to the threshold of the modern era, but World War II abruptly put this evolution on hold. It would be five years by the calendar and *many* years by the yardstick of technological progress before the process would begin again.

THE ORIGIN OF AIR TRAVEL

Air travel itself had, of course, begun on the first day that the Wright brothers carried a passenger in one of their Flyers, but the dream of airplanes flying actual routes and keeping to a scheduled timetable did not come into reality until after World War I.

As would be the case a generation later with World War II, the 1914–1918 war had been good for aviation. When it began, aviation was considered to be an interesting novelty, but the war years saw a refinement in the reliability and performance of airframes, as well as an improvement in "aero engine" technology. The sputtering four-cylinder engines of the early days were replaced by thundering V-8s and eventually by huge radial engines with more than a dozen cylinders.

More power and better airplanes meant more speed and maneuverability for the classic dogfights, but engineers were also working on an improvement in range and altitude that would make profitable commercial aviation a reality after the war. Before the war, there were no real airlines. In the early twenties, airlines seemed to be cropping up everywhere, especially in Europe and North America. Some were organized to connect only two or three cities, and these eventually faded away, but others began with—or quickly adopted—a vision of a truly comprehensive air transport network. A good example is the national flag carrier of the Netherlands, Koninklijke Luchtvaart Maatschappij (KLM, Royal Dutch Airlines), which began in the early twenties with a few domestic routes and a flight from Amsterdam to London. Today, KLM is a major worldwide carrier.

By 1939 many of the airlines that are familiar to us today were flying routes that still form the heart of their service areas. In Europe there was KLM, as well as Swissair, Finnair, Deutsche Luft Hansa (now known simply as Lufthansa), and the original British Airways. The last mentioned, which had been formed in 1937 by a merger of three smaller airlines in Britain, would eventually evolve into the company of the same name that has existed since 1972.

In the United States, there were Delta Air Lines, United Air Lines, Northwest Airlines, and American Airlines, as well as TWA—which was then Transcontinental & Western Airlines, not yet Trans-World Airlines. Such great, gone, but not forgotten, giants as Eastern Airlines and Pan American World Airways were also well established by 1939.

As the airlines evolved, and as the traveling public began to take air travel seriously, aircraft manufacturers began to compete to build better airliners. In 1919 air travel might have meant climbing into an open cockpit with your suitcase on your lap for an ear-splitting ride in the prop-wash of a vibrating engine. By the late thirties, airlines offered enclosed cabins, seats with at least some pretense of comfort, and enough soundproofing that you could carry on a conversation with your fellow passengers. Most of the major airlines had begun to offer meal service on porcelain dishware and some even offered sleeping accommodations.

As airlines and potential passengers started to get serious about air transport as a viable service, aircraft builders started getting serious about building aircraft to meet their needs. Boeing was developing its modern Model 247 airliner for its sister company, Boeing Air Transport (which was spun off as United Air Lines in 1934). Meanwhile, the competition—specifically Transcontinental & Western Air—had noticed what was happening at United. In order to compete successfully with United, TWA would also need to compete with the Boeing 247.

In August 1932, Jack Frye, the vice president for operations at TWA, wrote to the major planemakers, requesting a bid on ten airliners of a new design. He wanted this new design to be fast, reliable, and capable of crossing the Rocky Mountains safely. If any aircraft could be designed to do this, Frye would pay for ten examples in gold. Douglas Aircraft Company accepted the challenge and put its best designers to work on the project.

Although Boeing's 247 was delivered sooner, Douglas finished the prototype DC-1 in less than a year. The big silver bird was larger than the 247, and, after initial engine problems were overcome, she flew beautifully. The DC-1 first flew on July 1, 1933, and was delivered to TWA on September 13, 1933. It carried 12 passengers and had a range of 998 miles, and Frye was so delighted that TWA placed an order for 25 more production planes. They would differ slightly from the DC-1 and would be delivered under the designation DC-2. The DC-2 first flew on May 11, 1934, and the first airline delivery was to TWA two days later. The DC-2 was almost identical to the DC-1, but it was faster, could carry more passengers, and had a longer range.

Placed into service between Chicago and Newark an unprecedented two days after its delivery flight, the first DC-2 actually broke the speed record for that route *four times* in just over a week. The DC-2 was also promptly exported to Europe, as KLM was the second customer after TWA to buy the aircraft. After a KLM DC-2 came in second in the October 1934 MacRobertson London-to-Melbourne Air Race, commercial orders poured in from around the world.

The plane's reputation was such that the DC-2 won company owner Donald Douglas the 1936 Collier Trophy for aviation achievement—presented personally by President Roosevelt—and solidly launched his company into the world of commercial aviation. After 156 DC-2s, Douglas turned to a similar but larger and improved version.

As Jack Frye had been the catalyst for the DC-1/DC-2, C. R. Smith of American Airlines helped to make the next generation possible. In 1934 he went to Douglas with the idea for a transcontinental airliner with sleeping berths such as the railroads offered. The resulting aircraft, with a wider fuselage than the DC-2, was the Douglas Skysleeper Transport (DST), which first flew on December 17, 1935. That day, the 32nd anniversary of the Wright Brothers' first flight, was significant for another aviation milestone of almost equal importance.

The DST, which was redesignated as DC-3 when configured as a day-use nonsleeper offered luxury and reliability that could not have been imagined only a few years before. In fact, the DST offered better accommodations than one gets today. It could carry varying numbers of passengers depending on its internal arrangement, but typically the number was 21 in regular seating, or 14 in the DST sleeper configuration with sleeping accommodations. Its "Sky Room" was literally a suite with a private bath. The DST/DC-3 revolutionized air travel, and then, suddenly, there was a war.

THE POSTWAR QUARTER CENTURY

A growing segment of the traveling public had had a taste of air travel before World War II, but this was really just a preview. In the late thirties, middle distance passengers experienced the satisfaction of diminished travel time on flights between London and Paris and between New York and Washington, but the DC-3 and aircraft of its generation were still considerably slower on long flights than four-engine transport aircraft would be. On paper, they weren't that much slower, but for a passenger who had to cool his or her heels in Omaha or Albuquerque while the DC-3 was being refueled, the time slipped away. The four-engine transport aircraft would revolutionize the public's perception of distance.

When the evolution of commercial aviation emerged from its wartime hibernation in 1945, the traveling public in Europe, Australia, and North America were ready to start taking it seriously. With the advent of long-range, four-engine aircraft, the airlines would be much more able to compete with the railroads.

What did the four-engine transport aircraft offer to the traveling public that had never been offered before? They offered speed, which, of course, translated as time. With refueling stops, twin-engine aircraft lost precious time, but the new generation of larger aircraft could make the same trip in half the time simply by eliminating some or all of the refueling stops.

A trip that once took all night and part of a day by train—or most of a day in a twin-engine airliner—could be accomplished in an afternoon. A traveler setting out to travel coast to coast by train would have had to set aside the better part of a week. In a DC-3, several refueling stops would force the loss of the better part of two days. A four-engine airliner could fly from coast to coast in the United States in a single day—with one, and eventually no, refueling stop.

Another very important way that the four-engine transport aircraft shortened distances and changed civilization was in intercontinental travel. In this regard, the traveling public had also had a small taste in the last years before the war. Nonstop flights across the Atlantic had been headline grabbers in the twenties, and airline flights across the "pond" were just barely becoming routine on the eve of World War II. The same was true of flights between England and the important outposts of the British Empire. In the late thirties, Pan American World Airways had begun regular transatlantic and transpacific service with its "Clipper" flying boats—notably the Boeing 314, and British Overseas Airways Corporation (BOAC) was scheduling flights to South Africa, India, and Australia with its "Empire" class of flying boats. These great aircraft were the first generation of practical four-engine transport aircraft, but they did not use airports, and many important population centers did not have a convenient body of water for seaplane use.

In this book, we discuss two generations of American airliners. The first are the great postwar propliners, the second are the first generation of jetliners. The latter were the first of their kind. They were born at a time when virtually nothing like them had ever existed, yet they firmly defined what

a jetliner should be. Indeed, the forward fuselage and cabin cross-section that Boeing designed in the early fifties for its first jetliner was still in production at the turn of the century in the successive generations of 737s. The fuselages may have varied in length, but the width has not. As for the Douglas DC-9, we saw the company name change twice since it was introduced, but the DC-9 is still in production—ironically as the Boeing 717.

In 1945 the era of the classic airliners saw the end of one epoch, but the beginning of another that is still very much with us. Aircraft technology was evolving by leaps and bounds, and the world—especially the United States—was ready for the big propliners.

THE AIRPORTS

During the two decades that followed World War II, the economy in the United States was the strongest in the world, and this boom cycle fueled major cultural changes. One of the most important was in the perception of travel.

One of the aspects most overlooked in the history of aviation is the development of airports. In the early days of aviation, airports were called airfields and they were literally fields. Paved runways, a novelty in 1930, were getting to be fairly commonplace by 1940, but most were not long enough to accommodate four-engine transport aircraft, so most four-engine transport aircraft were flying boats. The leaps in aviation technology were resulting in aircraft that were too big for existing airports, so the airports had to grow.

Among the billions that were spent on aviation by the U.S. government during World War II, a great deal was earmarked for airport improvement. The American war effort built new aircraft by the tens of thousands, but a more lasting legacy would be in the hundreds of new paved runway airfields that were built as training fields, not to mention the enormous improvements to major airports that already existed. When the war was over, thousands of airplanes were cut up for scrap, or discarded as unnecessary, but the airports remained, ready for the future and for a new generation of airplanes.

CHAPTER ONE

THE DOUGLAS DC-4:

The First with Four

The first commercially successful American four-engine landplane propliner was the Douglas DC-4. While its commercial success would not come until after World War II, it was conceived and first flown before the war, and the first production series DC-4s were on the assembly line in Santa Monica, California, in December 1941 when the Japanese bombed Pearl Harbor.

By the late thirties, the DC-3 was proving itself, and the future of safe, reliable air travel was clearly in sight. As the traveling public accepted air travel, more and more people, naturally, wanted to fly. In order to meet this increasing demand, the airlines, naturally, wanted larger aircraft with more passenger capacity and longer range. This meant four engines instead of two or three.

Both Martin and Sikorsky had produced four-engine seaplanes for Pan American in 1934, and Short Brothers in England began producing its Empire class seaplanes in 1934. Boeing's Model 314 Clipper, a much larger and more sophisticated four-engine, flying boat seaplane, would come onto the scene in 1938, but four-engine landplane development lagged behind.

Throughout the thirties, most of the landplanes that were built with four engines—anywhere in the world—were either military aircraft destined for development as long-range bombers or reconnaissance aircraft, or they were demonstrators that would never evolve into production aircraft.

Partly, the lag in large landplane development was a function of factors so mundane as a lack of airports. In the 1920s most landplanes operated from airfields that were literally fields. It was not until the thirties that cities in Europe and North America began to invest in paved runways specifically dedicated to use by scheduled airlines.

Gradually, as the market for air travel improved, so did the airports and other infrastructure designed to meet the needs of the airlines. As this occurred, and as the airlines began to express an interest, airframe builders began to design larger aircraft. In Seattle, Boeing borrowed design features from its four-engine B-17 bomber and began work on the Model 307 Stratoliner, but the company that had brought the world the DC-3 was one step ahead.

A top view of the triple-tailed DC-4E in Douglas livery. Larger than the DC-4 that would go into service after World War II, the one-of-a-kind DC-4E was sold to Japan and never used commercially in the United States.

The Douglas DC-4E in United Air Lines markings at New York's Floyd Bennett Field during her June 1939 publicity tour. The tour made the public aware that Douglas was building a four-engine airliner, but the single-tailed production-model DC-4 was quite a different bird from the DC-4E.

The Douglas Aircraft Company had started development of the DC-4 even before the DC-3 made its maiden flight in 1937. Just as Jack Frye of TWA and C. R. Smith of American Airlines had provided the impetus for the DC-1 and DC-3, it was W. A. "Pat" Patterson of United Air Lines that got the

DC-4 program off the ground. Then, in an unprecedented move, four other major American air carriers —American, Eastern, Pan American, and TWA— also approached Douglas jointly in early 1936, offering to invest in the development costs. The new aircraft that they had in mind would have twice the passenger capacity and twice the range of the DC-3. This meant a propliner that could fly routinely for 2,500 miles without a refueling stop—including flights between Labrador and Europe across the once-for-midable North Atlantic. An ordinary passenger would be able to accomplish the feat that had made Charles Lindbergh a hero just ten years before—and in less time.

The prototype made its first flight on June 7, 1938. Designated as the DC-4E, with the E for "experimental," the aircraft was indeed an experiment. Only one DC-4E was built, intended as a proof of concept demonstrator and not actually a production prototype. It was designed with a triple tail and was larger than the production DC-4 would be. The DC-4E had a wingspan of 138 feet 3 inches, and a length of 97 feet

The Douglas DC-4E in flight with her number one prop feathered. The DC-4E was seen in both Douglas and United Air Lines markings, but it would never actually fly in routine airline service.

4 inches. It weighed 66,500 pounds fully loaded and fueled, and had a service ceiling of 22,900 feet. It was powered by four 1,450-horsepower, air-cooled, 14-cylinder Pratt & Whitney R-2180-S1A-G radial engines that gave it a cruising speed of 245 miles per hour at 7,000 feet.

The DC-4E had a range of 2,200 miles and was designed to accommodate 42 seated passengers, or 30 in sleeping compartments. Like the earlier Douglas DST, it had a *bridal suite*. In contrast to the sleep-in-your-seat passenger accommodations to which we have grown accustomed in the last quarter of the twentieth century, the large airliners of the thirties and forties were designed by and for people who were used to traveling in the Pullman sleeping cars. It never occurred to the airliner designers of the thirties and forties *not* to at least offer the option of proper sleeping arrangements for passengers traveling a thousand miles or more.

During the spring of 1939, the DC-4E was painted in the livery of a United Air Lines "Mainliner" and flown extensively, while Douglas refined the design of the production series DC-4s. At the end of the year, the DC-4E was sold to Greater Japan Airlines (Nippon Koku) and was later reported to have crashed into Tokyo Bay. In fact, it was delivered to the Japanese aircraft maker Nakajima, who would use it as the prototype for the G5N bomber that would be used in small numbers during World War II. In an ironic footnote, a conventional DC-4 would be the first aircraft to be operated by Japan Airlines when the carrier was reconstituted in 1952, seven years after Japan's defeat in World War II.

By 1939, meanwhile, both TWA and Pan American had pulled out of the DC-4 consortium to commit themselves to acquiring the Boeing 307 Stratoliner, which had made its debut on the last day of 1938. The 307 also had four engines and greater range than a DC-3, and it had a pressurized cabin—unlike the DC-3 or the DC-4. The Stratoliner was about 20 percent smaller than the production DC-4s would be, and it was perceived as being less mechanically complex. Ultimately, it would be less commercially successful.

Boeing would receive only ten orders for its Stratoliner—five from TWA, four from Pan American, and one from the millionaire film producer and aviation enthusiast, Howard Hughes. Douglas, however, soon had 50 orders on its books from United, American, and Eastern.

The urgency felt by the American carriers to get a long-range airliner into service *soon* was prompted in

Douglas C-54 and DC-4 wing sections are seen here at the Santa Monica, California, factory where Douglas would build more than 1,200 of this airframe type.

part by the successful 4,075-mile, Berlin-to-New York flight of a Focke-Wulf Fw 200 belonging to Germany's Deutsche Luft Hansa in August 1938. The Fw 200 would eventually see limited service as an airliner, but would be used extensively in its true and intended role—as a long-range patrol bomber—during World War II.

The production variant of the Douglas propliner, initially designated as DC-4A, but generally known simply as DC-4, was smaller than the DC-4E and had a single vertical tail. It had a wingspan of 117 feet 6 inches—nearly 21 feet less than the DC-4E. It was 93 feet 10 inches long—almost four feet shorter than the DC-4E. It weighed 73,000 pounds fully loaded and fueled, and had a ferry range of 2,500 miles. It was powered by four air-cooled, 14-cylinder Pratt & Whitney R-2000-3 Twin Wasp radial engines. The DC-4A would be capable of carrying varying numbers of passengers depending on its internal arrangement, and this ranged from 50 to 80, more than double the capacity of the DC-3, and substantially more than the Stratoliner, which carried 33 in a typical configuration.

The DC-4As were nearing completion when the United States entered World War II at the end of 1941. While the war years would be good for aviation in general because of the government-sponsored leaps in

A DC-4 destined for National Airlines is seen here as it nears completion on the Douglas factory floor at Santa Monica, California. After World War II, the fourth commercial DC-4 delivery was to National.

technology, they arrested the development of commercial aviation. Commercial DC-4s were supposed to be flying the airways in 1942, but instead, the USAAF recognized their value as military transports, commandeered the 24 American and United ships that were then on the assembly line, and put them into service as military transports under the designation C-54.

The first 24 DC-4As had almost been completed—with their civilian standard interiors mostly installed—and these became simply "C-54s" with no series suffix. The remaining 26 that were on the books from the commercial orders were not yet in final assembly, so there was an opportunity for modification, especially involving the strengthening of their floors for heavy cargo. These aircraft would be completed as C-54As. In addition, the USAAF increased its order to a total of 252 C-54A aircraft, which were given the official name "Skymaster." Of these, 97

would be built at the original Douglas plant at Santa Monica, and the rest at new factory near Chicago, which evolved into today's O'Hare International Airport. The first C-54, which had been intended to be the first production commercial DC-4A, made its maiden flight on February 14, 1942.

During 1942 and 1943, the USAAF placed a series of orders for aircraft that would be similar to the C-54As, but with provisions for stretcher racks that would be used in evacuating severely wounded personnel from the war zones to hospitals in the United States. These aircraft, which could also be fitted with seats for use as conventional troop transports, also were built with larger wing tanks and were designated C-54B. A total of 100 C-54Bs were built in Santa Monica and 120 in Chicago.

The next major C-54 variant was the C-54D, which was similar to the C-54B, but was equipped with Pratt & Whitney R-2000-11 Twin Wasps, delivering 1,350 horsepower. There were 380 C-54Ds completed in Chicago. Next came the C-54E, of which 125 were built in Santa Monica. These were similar to the C-54D, but they had increased fuel capacity and provisions for fast conversion between a passenger interior and a cargo-carrying interior. The C-54F designation was assigned to a troop transport variant that was never produced, and the C-54G designation went to 162 Santa Monica-built C-54E airframes that were equipped with 1,500-horsepower Pratt & Whitney R-2000-9 Twin Wasps.

Meanwhile, the missing "C-54C" designation was assigned to a single C-54A, which was converted to an executive transport. It was also given a "V" prefix for "Very Important Person," for the executive that it was to carry was President Franklin Delano Roosevelt. Converted in 1944, and given the official nickname

and call sign *Sacred Cow*, the VC-54C was America's first presidential aircraft, the forerunner of today's Air Force One. The interior contained a presidential stateroom, a meeting room, and accommodations for the president's staff.

President Roosevelt, who preferred to travel at sea aboard naval vessels—or by train when in the United States—used the *Sacred Cow* only for his trip to Yalta in the Crimea in February 1945 for his summit conference with Soviet leader Josef Stalin and Britain's Prime Minister Winston Churchill. The Prime Minister, meanwhile, had a C-54B, which he used more extensively during the war. Churchill's C-54B was one of 23 such aircraft that were transferred to the Royal Air Force during the war. They served under the designation Skymaster I and were returned to the USAAF after 1945.

The first commercial Douglas DC-4A is seen here as it appeared in "factory fresh" condition before it was turned over to the USAAF as the first C-54. The first batch of DC-4As were on the Santa Monica assembly line when the Japanese bombed Pearl Harbor, and they were all diverted to the USAAF. Note the newly cut large cargo door.

The U.S. Navy also used the C-54, giving it the designation R5D, meaning that it was the fifth Douglas-made transport type operated by the Navy. The USAAF acquired all of these from Douglas under C-54 designations and then transferred them to the Navy. There were 57 C-54As that became R5D-1s, 30 C-54Bs that became R5D-2s, and 95 C-54Ds that became R5D-3s.

An early Douglas C-54A, the USAAF transport based on the DC-4, circa 1942. All of the commercial DC-4s under construction when the United States entered World War II were drafted into USAAF service, but the USAAF had ordered more than two dozen of its own before the end of 1941.

The long-delayed debut of the DC-4 as a commercial airliner came at last—nearly two months after World War II officially ended. A DC-4 belonging to American Overseas Airlines—a subsidiary of American Airlines—made the historic flight from New York, touching down at Hurn Airport, near Bournemouth, England, on October 24, 1945. The flight was historic on another count as well. In the days of heavy regulation of the American airline industry, the Civil Aeronautics Administration (CAA) limited the number of airlines that could be American overseas flag carriers. The October 24 flight marked the first such flight since the CAA ended the monopoly previously enjoyed by Pan American, by extending to American and TWA the right to carry the American flag across the Atlantic.

After the war, an expanding North American economy and a pent-up desire for travel would lead to a rapidly growing market for modern airliners. In terms of marketing, the DC-4—albeit in the olive-drab uniform of the C-54 series—had already become successful beyond the Douglas Aircraft Company's dreams. After the war, Douglas had every reason to suppose that commercial sales

would resume as if there had been no interruption. However, the new DC-4s that the company could now produce for the commercial market now faced serious competition from the hundreds of surplus C-54s that were now flooding the market at costs substantially below what it would cost for a new one from the factory.

Nevertheless, Douglas would receive orders for 79 factory-new commercial DC-4s, the last of which would be delivered on August 9, 1947. The careers of these aircraft, along with their military surplus sisters, would last for decades.

As the most well-established four-engine airliner in the world, the DC-4/C-54 family was in demand by nearly every airline with a route structure that could justify putting it into service. Within a year of the end of the war, the four-motored Douglases were not an uncommon sight over the important cities of Europe and North America, as well as South America, the Far East, and points between. In February 1946, an Australian DC-4 became the first commercial DC-4 to open a scheduled route across the Pacific, connecting Sydney with Vancouver, British Columbia, via San Francisco, Hawaii, and Fiji.

Through the first spring and summer after the war, European airlines followed the lead of the Americans in opening new routes across the North Atlantic using DC-4s. Typically, these flights terminated at New York City, with a refueling stop in Gander, Newfoundland. The first European carrier on the North Atlantic was the Netherlands' KLM, which opened its service from Amsterdam's Schiphol Airport in May 1945, followed by Air France out of Paris in June. The Scandinavian Airlines System (SAS) began DC-4 service from Stockholm in July. Of the customers for new, postwar-built DC-4s, Air France would be the largest, with orders for 15 aircraft, followed by Belgium's flag carrier, Sabena, which took delivery of nine.

Domestically, DC-4s were in service with United and Eastern, as well as with other carriers, such as Capital, which was the first to offer DC-4 all-coach-class service in the United States—between New York and Chicago in November 1948. By configuring the DC-4s for 60 passengers, Capital was able to sell its seats for four cents a mile rather than the usual six cents.

An Eastern Airlines DC-4. Before World War II, Eastern had been one of the launch customers for the DC-4 program, but the carrier had to wait four years to get its airplanes.

It is also worth noting that it was a DC-4—belonging to Peruvian International Airways—that had the distinction of being the first scheduled, commercial flight to land at New York's Idlewild (John F. Kennedy International after 1963) Airport, when the sprawling facility replaced LaGuardia as New York's primary airport on July 31, 1948. Another milestone achieved by the DC-4 came on December 12, 1951, when an Alaska Airlines DC-4 became the first commercial airliner to fly across the North Pole.

A considerably darker footnote to the DC-4's career occurred on November 1, 1949, when an Eastern Airlines DC-4 was involved in a midair collision that would result in 55 fatalities—the greatest number yet recorded in a civil air disaster. The DC-4 was struck over Washington National Airport by a P-38 fighter.

Other DC-4s would figure in some of the tense moments of the Cold War. In April 1952, an Air France DC-4 was fired on by Soviet aircraft during its final approach to Berlin's Tempelhof Airport, and in July 1954, a Cathay Pacific DC-4 was shot down by Chinese interceptors over the South China Sea.

While many of the C-54 and R5D aircraft were sold as military surplus at the end of World War II, a large number also remained in service with the U.S. Navy and the U.S. Air Force (USAAF until 1948) well into the 1960s. More than 30 C-54Ds and C-54Es were converted for use in air-sea rescue operations under the designations SC-54D and SC-54E, and 30 C-54Es were converted to MC-54Ms for medical evacuation duties in 1951 during the worst months of the Korean War. Nine C-54Ds were converted for use

in missile tracking and recovery operations during the early sixties under the designation JC-54D.

One of the most heroic applications for postwar military Skymasters fell to the C-54Ms—38 early-model C-54s that were modified as flying coal hoppers. When the Soviet Union blockaded Berlin during the winter of 1948–1949, the only way to supply the beleaguered city was by air, and this meant that even coal had to be flown in. Of course, the Berlin Airlift also saw many other British and American Skymasters carrying food, medicine, and other supplies into the city.

Despite the modifications and variations, all of the DC-4 and C-54 series aircraft that were delivered between 1942 and 1947 retained the same basic airframe and were powered by Pratt & Whitney R-2000 series Twin Wasp engines. In the meantime, however, Douglas was experimenting with a substantially improved four-engine transport that would be based on the DC-4/C-54. During World War II, Douglas proposed a series of these to the USAAF as C-54 replacements.

In 1944, Douglas had presented the idea of a pressurized development of the C-54E, with larger

A Pan American DC-4, converted from a USAAF C-54 (note the cargo door), circa 1957. Pan American did not buy any DC-4s directly from Douglas. Instead, it picked up used C-54s, converted these, and waited for new DC-6s.

Swissair acquired four DC-4s from Douglas. The national flag carrier of Switzerland was one of the last of the European operators of the type to place its orders with Douglas. Before World War II, it had been mainly a regional carrier, and overseas routes were not quick in coming for the cautious Swiss.

rectangular windows in place of the familiar circular portholes. The fuselage would be seven feet longer and the powerplants would be four Pratt & Whitney R-2800-34 radial engines, each delivering 2,100 horsepower. The USAAF ordered one prototype under the designation XC-112 and a service test aircraft designated YC-112. The XC-112 made its first flight on February 15, 1946, but by that time, the war was over and the YC-112 had been cancelled. However, rather than being an end to a story, the XC-112 marked the beginning of one of the most commercially successful Douglas Commercial programs, the DC-6. Indeed, from a design point of view, the XC-112 was the first DC-6.

Also during World War II, the USAAF assigned designations to three other Douglas proposals for three other aircraft that were suggested to evolve from C-54 modifications. All of these involved replacing the Pratt & Whitney air-cooled radial engines with water-cooled inline engines, and none of the three was actually built. The XC-114 would have used four Allison V-1710 engines, and the XC-115 would have had four Packard Merlin V-1650-209 engines. The Merlin was used by Supermarine in the legendary Spitfire fighter aircraft, and the Packard

Merlin, based on the Rolls-Royce Merlin, was the engine that was used by the North American P-51 Mustang, the top American fighter of the war. The XC-116 would have used Allison V-1710s like the XC-114, but with thermal deicers.

The Rolls-Royce Merlin, meanwhile, would play an important role in an important variant of the DC-4, and the only major version of a Douglas Commercial propliner to be built under license abroad, the Canadair North Star.

The idea for the North Star dated back to 1943, when the Canadian government decided on the ambitious plan of producing a four-engine transport in Canada for the Royal Canadian Air Force that would also be available after the war for use by the state-owned Trans-Canada Airways. The decision was made to license an existing American make rather than developing the aircraft from the ground up in Canada. The Douglas DC-4 was chosen over the Lockheed Constellation because the DC-4 was already in production as the C-54. The obvious choice for a powerplant would have been the Pratt & Whitney R-2000 series Twin Wasp, but for political reasons, the Canadian government—as a member of the British Commonwealth—decided to select the British Rolls-Royce Merlin.

In 1944 a license arrangement was negotiated with Douglas, whereby a C-54G-standard aircraft would be produced by Canadair at Cartierville, Quebec, near Montreal, under the designation C-54GM for Royal Canadian Air Force or the DC-4M for the commercial market, with the "M" indicating the

A Douglas DC-4 in the markings of Swedish Airlines, which was later incorporated into the Scandinavian Airlines System (SAS). A trinational consortium that also includes Norway and Denmark, SAS would be a loyal customer of Douglas (later McDonnell Douglas) equipment up through the MD-80 series.

engine choice. The commercial designation was later abbreviated to C-4. The terms of the license stipulated that Canadair could not sell the aircraft outside Canada and the United Kingdom in markets where they might compete with potential Douglas sales.

Originally, Canadair was to build a total of 70 C-54GM/DC-4Ms, with 50 going to the Royal Canadian Air Force and the remainder to Trans-Canada Airways. However, with the war obviously nearing an end, the military cut its order to 24. With this in mind, it was also decided that the initial deliveries would be to the airline rather than to the military as originally planned. The first six aircraft were assembled from completed fuselages and other components that were manufactured by Douglas in Chicago, but the remainder would be built entirely by Canadair. Most of these would be built after the debut of the DC-6, so they would take advantage of certain DC-6 components, such as landing gear, which permitted an increased gross weight.

The first DC-4M made its maiden flight on July 15, 1946, having been christened "North Star," a name with a double meaning that implied that the aircraft was a "star" from the "north," and it also made reference to Polaris, the North Star, which is often used in celestial navigation. Trans-Canada Airways took delivery of the first North Star on November 16, 1946, but it did not begin carrying passengers on the

Transatlantic route until April 15, 1947. When the North Star did begin to fly, it racked up an impressive record right out of the chute, making 58 Atlantic crossings in its first 58 days. Over the course its first year, the North Star would set three speed records for flights between Canada and European destinations.

The Merlin engines gave the North Star its speed and durability, but they were also to provide the aircraft with its primary developmental problem. They were powerful, but they were much noisier than the Wasps used in the DC-4 and the inboard engines vented exhaust directly against the passenger cabin. Attempts to alleviate this problem were only partially successful.

If the Merlins created a problem for those riding in the North Star, they created an opportunity for those marketing the North Star. Britain, whose industrial base was still reeling from the effects of the war, wanted to protect its indigenous aircraft manufacturers from competition. This meant that state-owned enterprises from the Royal Air Force to the flag-carrying airline, British Overseas Airway Corporation (BOAC), would be expected to "buy British." Canadair wanted to sell North Stars to BOAC, and BOAC wanted them. The North Stars were Canadian copies of American aircraft—but they had British engines, so BOAC was able to buy the aircraft.

BOAC wanted the North Star simply because the British aviation industry had failed to come up with an

A Douglas DC-4 in the livery of Suid Afrikaanse Lugdiens (South African Airways), circa 1947. The flag carrier of the largest airline based on the continent would ultimately buy five DC-4s from Douglas.

alternative. The Avro Tudor, which BOAC had been eyeing since it was proposed during World War II, proved to be unacceptable, and the Bristol Britannia, the four-engine airliner that it really wanted, would not be available for several years. BOAC took delivery of 22 North Stars, renaming them as C-4 Argonauts and using them extensively in the late 1940s and 1950s.

The Royal Canadian Air Force accepted its first North Star into No. 426 Squadron on September 12, 1947, and flew its fleet for nearly 200 million miles—during the Korean War and in conjunction with United Nations peacekeeping operations worldwide—without a fatality. The last Royal Canadian Air Force North Star was retired on December 8, 1965. The air force purchased one additional North Star as an executive transport, to replace one that had been lost while it was on loan to Trans-Canada Airways. This one was designated as a C-5 North Star and was powered by Pratt & Whitney R-2800, rather than Merlin, engines.

Trans-Canada Airways continued to operate the North Star for many years, although in 1955, the fleet was changed to all-economy class, increasing capacity from 52 to 62 passengers.

At the same time that BOAC was taking delivery of its Argonaut fleet, Canadian Pacific Airways purchased four C-4 Argonauts for its own transocean routes. These brought the total number of North Stars produced by Canadair to 70.

At Douglas, the production totals stood at 80 commercial DC-4s, including the DC-4E, and 1,162 C-54s and R5Ds. Of these aircraft, 586 were produced in Santa Monica and the rest in Chicago.

By the early 1950s, the DC-4 had been retired from the transatlantic routes that it had pioneered during the 1940s, and by mid-decade, it had been replaced by more advanced aircraft—including the DC-6—in the service of the major scheduled carriers who had once celebrated it as a milestone. The DC-4 would remain, however, with freight carriers and small regional charter carriers through the end of the century.

In terms of production totals, the DC-4 (and its military derivatives) is second only to the DC-3 (and its military derivatives) among the Douglas propliners. The DC-4 will always be remembered as the first modern airliner of the postwar era.

Japan Airlines was an operator of pre-owned Douglas DC-4 aircraft. Because of postwar restrictions, Japan was forbidden to have a national airline until the mid-1950s, and the first aircraft that it operated were acquired on the used aircraft market.

A Douglas DC-4 being prepped for delivery to Societe Anonym Belge d'Exploitation de la Navigation Aerienne (Sabena). Belgium's flag carrier was the largest European customer that Douglas would have for the DC-4 program.

CHAPTER TWO

THE DC-6 AND DC-7:

The Last Douglas Propliners

The DC-6 was essentially the DC-4 redesigned with the benefit of the experience that the Douglas Aircraft Company had gained dur- ingWorld War II. It was a commercial product developed in response to the Lockheed Model 49 Constellation, which was clearly supe- rior to the DC-4. Like the DC-4, the Constellation had been designed before the war as a four-engine airliner, but had not reached the airlines before the war. It had first flown in January 1943 and had been drafted into military service. Lockheed had raised the ante on Dou- glas, but because of the war, there would be no airline deliveries, so Douglas had until the war ended to come up with an airplane to raise the ante on the Model 49.

Meanwhile, the USAAF was constantly looking for improvements to existing aircraft. As an improvement to the C-54, the military vari- ant of the DC-4, Douglas had proposed the pressurized version with four Pratt & Whitney R-2800-34 radial engines that the USAAF desig- nated XC-112. A single example of this aircraft was produced by lengthening a C-54E fuselage by seven feet and pressurizing it, but by the time the XC-112 prototype was completed in 1946, the war was over, so there were no immediate military production orders. The experience of producing the prototype gave Douglas a head start on the DC-6, however, just as the commercial DC-4 had given the USAAF a head start on a four-engine transport at the beginning of the war.

The first flight of the XC-112 on February 15, 1946, was closely watched by two of the original DC-4 customers, American Airlines and United Air Lines. They placed orders for 50 and 20, respectively, to be delivered under the Douglas Commercial designation DC-6.

The DC-6 was to the DC-4 what the DC-3 had been to the DC-2. It was similar in appearance at first glance, but the circular porthole win- dows were replaced by the larger, rounded-corner rectangular windows. Inside, the lengthened cabin allowed for 20 percent more passengers— up to 100—and the pressurization made it possible to fly above the weather, giving those passengers a smoother and more comfortable ride. The DC-6 had a wingspan of 117 feet 6 inches (the same as the DC-4), and a length of 105 feet 7 inches. It weighed 107,000 pounds fully loaded and fueled and had a service ceiling of 25,000 feet. The engines were four Pratt & Whitney R-2800 radials, each rated at 2,100 horsepower.

The first commercial DC-6 deliveries were made to American Airlines and United Air Lines simultaneously in a festive ceremony held on March 28, 1947. United, however, was the first to put its new aircraft to work, with a debut on April 27 of coast-to-coast service between San

A Douglas DC-6B in the livery of Northwest Airlines. The Minnesota-based carrier had been an early supporter of Boeing's Stratocruiser, but they also bought nearly a dozen DC-6Bs.

A Douglas DC-6 in the markings of a United Air Lines Mainliner over the Pacific coast with the Golden Gate Bridge and the city of San Francisco in the distance. In the 1950s, San Francisco was America's key gateway for transpacific flights.

Francisco and New York. The DC-6 was capable of making this nonstop flight in 10 hours, compared to 14 for the DC-4 or 11 for the rival Lockheed Constellation.

In the meanwhile, the USAAF also placed an order for a DC-6, not under the C-112 designation that had been used for the original progenitor of the DC-6 lineage, but under a new designation, VC-118. This aircraft, ordered in 1946, was earmarked to be the second officially designated executive transport for the president of the United States. Unlike the retrofitted VC-54C known as *Sacred Cow*, which had served President Roosevelt briefly in 1945 and President Truman during 1945 and 1946, the VC-118 was the first aircraft that was factory-built for an American president, as is the case with today's Air Force One aircraft.

The VC-118 was designed with a presidential stateroom, 25 executive seats, and sleeping accommodations for 14 persons in addition to the president. The aircraft was delivered on July 1, 1947, and was nicknamed *Independence*, after President Harry Truman's hometown in Missouri.

In the closing weeks of 1947, cabin fires aboard two commercial DC-6s forced a grounding of the entire DC-6 fleet on November 12. First, a United DC-6 crashed at Bryce Canyon, Utah, killing all 52 people aboard, and then an American DC-6 caught fire over New Mexico. In the latter incident, the pilot was able to make a successful emergency landing. Douglas engineers diagnosed the problem—a fuel overflow being sucked into a cabin heater duct—and corrective procedures were undertaken. On March 21, 1948, a year after the first DC-6 deliveries, the aircraft were given a clean bill of health by the Civil Aeronautics Administration.

Even as Douglas was working to correct problems on the DC-6, the company was working on new, upgraded versions. These were the DC-6A, a dedicated cargo variant that made its first flight on September

29, 1949, and a new passenger variant, which would be designated DC-6B. This aircraft, which first flew on February 10, 1951, would eventually evolve into the standard production model of the DC-6 series.

Five feet longer than a DC-6, it offered a 7 percent increase in passenger capacity, with just a 4 percent increase in operating costs. The DC-6B was powered by four 2,400 horsepower, air-cooled, 18-cylinder Pratt & Whitney R-2800-CB16 or 2,500 horsepower R-2800-CB17 Double Wasp engines that gave it a cruising speed of 315 miles per hour. Its range was 3,000 miles, easily sufficient for flying coast-to-coast across the United States without fueling stops.

The first DC-6B went into service with United Air Lines on April 11, 1951, just two months after the first flight, and the first DC-6A was delivered to Slick Airways on April 16. American Airlines, the other launch customer for the DC-6 four years earlier, placed an order with Douglas for six DC-6As and 17 DC-6Bs. The latter was, in turn, expanded to 41 in October. Meanwhile, the original DC-6 series would remain in production until the end of the year, with the last one being turned over to Braniff Airways on November 2, 1951, at Santa Monica.

The extended range of the DC-6B permitted routine commercial air service in places where it was not previously possible with commercial aircraft—notably across the Arctic. On November 16, 1954, a Scandinavian Airlines System (SAS) DC-6B arrived in Los Angeles after making the first scheduled flight between Europe and the West Coast of North America using the Polar Route. This pioneering passenger-carrying flight made stops in Greenland and at Winnipeg, Manitoba. It had been preceded by exploratory flights without passengers. On June 4, 1955, Canadian Airways joined SAS on the Polar Route with service between Amsterdam and Vancouver.

Many commercial aircraft systems that we now take for granted originated on the commercial aircraft of the 1950s. It was during 1955 that the DC-6B would help pioneer the use of a Bendix-developed radar system that permitted aircrews to track thunderstorms at night, an innovation that dramatically improved not only passenger comfort but passenger safety as well.

When the USAAF became independent of the U.S. Army as the U.S. Air Force in September 1947, there was a greater focus on disposing of surplus World War II aircraft than on acquiring new aircraft, especially for routine activities such as transportation.

The notion of an improved C-54, which had certainly seemed like a good idea when the XC-112 was proposed in 1944, was no longer a priority issue. When the war ended, there were more than enough C-54s to handle the USAAF's dramatically reduced requirements for air transport. When Douglas began producing the DC-6, the air force bought one as a presidential aircraft in 1947, but the VC-118 was a one-of-a-kind aircraft, and would remain so—that is, until the U.S. Air Force found itself at war in Korea.

When the war began in June 1950, the transport fleets of the U.S. Air Force's Military Air Transportation Service (MATS) and the U.S. Navy's Naval Air Transportation Service (NATS) were put to work carrying troops to the war zone and evacuating wounded personnel. Suddenly, the reduced fleet of four-engine transports—which consisted mainly of C-54s and R5Ds—was too little for the task.

In 1950 and early 1951, the U.S. Air Force ordered 101 C-118As for its own use, plus an additional 40 that would be loaned to the U.S. Navy for NATS use under the designation R6D-1. The U.S. Navy would subsequently increase its number of R6D-1s to 65 through direct acquisition from Douglas. It is worth

A Douglas DC-6 freighter in the livery of American Airlines in flight in May 1953. American took the DC-4 aircraft with the first dozen commercial serial numbers that Douglas would produce and added orders for 73 more. Ultimately, the 85 aircraft included freighters as well as passenger ships.

A passenger-configured Douglas DC-6 in the livery of a United Air Lines Mainliner during engine run-up. As the largest operator of passenger DC-6s, United bought 96 such aircraft from Douglas.

A Douglas DC-6 in United Air Lines livery with the staff and equipment of the carrier's maintenance base at San Francisco International Airport. This airport became an important hub for United Air Lines soon after World War II, and the United maintenance base at San Francisco is still one of the largest such facilities in the Western Hemisphere.

noting that in 1962, when the service designations were merged in 1962, all the R6D-1s still in service were designated as C-118B.

The C-118A/R6D-1 aircraft, which were given the name "Liftmaster" to distinguish them from the smaller C-54/R5D "Skymaster," were designed with accommodations for 74 fully equipped troops or 60 stretchers. The four engines were Pratt & Whitney R-2800-52W Double Wasps with 2,500 horsepower each.

The DC-6 series would remain in production for 11 years, from 1947, when the first two were completed for American and United, until November 17, 1958, when the 704th and last DC-6 airframe rolled

off the assembly line in Santa Monica. This aircraft was delivered to Jugoslovenski Aerotransport (JAT), the state airline of Yugoslavia.

Of the 704 DC-6 airframes, 537 went to commercial customers and 167 to the United States military. All 704 were produced at Santa Monica. The launch customers, United Air Lines and American Airlines, would also be the largest customers. Indeed, each airline launched its acquisition with an orders exceeding 40 aircraft. Ultimately, United would take 96 DC-6s and American 85.

Pan American World Airways bought 47, and its sister company, Panagra (Pan American Grace) added ten. Western Airlines acquired 31 and National Airlines ordered 16. Other customers in the United States included Braniff Airlines, Continental Airlines, Delta Air Lines, Los Angeles Air Service, Northeast Airlines, Northwest Airlines, Slick Airways.

Overseas, the Scandinavian Airlines System (SAS), which was to be one of the most loyal foreign customers for Douglas equipment through the years, acquired 31 DC-6s from the company. Sabena, Belgium's flag carrier, which had been a key DC-4 customer, ordered 16 DC-6s. The Belgian Air Force was also a customer. The national flag carrier of the Netherlands, Koninklijke Luchtvaart Maatschappij (KLM, Royal Dutch Airlines) also bought 16. Additional foreign DC-6 customers included Alitalia, All

A Douglas DC-6A passenger/cargo combination in the livery of charter carrier Overseas National Airways. Based in New Jersey, this second-tier carrier bought three DC-6Bs from Douglas, but picked up most of its equipment secondhand from United Air Lines.

A Douglas DC-6A in the markings of Alaska Airlines in flight in February 1958. Alaska did not buy any DC-6s directly from Douglas. In the 1950s, the carrier relied on the large numbers of pre-owned, but relatively new, aircraft on the market.

The cable cars on San Francisco's Nob Hill shared billing with a Douglas DC-6 in this 1954 United Air Lines ad for packaged tours. The DC-6 is not identified as such. With this ad, United was selling a destination, not equipment.

Nippon Airways, Canadian Pacific, Ethiopian Airlines, LAN-Chile, Maritime Central of Canada, Mexicana, Swissair, and Trans Caribbean. Other users ranged from the Arabian-American Oil Company (Aramco) to the Hunting Clan in Great Britain.

The early fifties were a critical time in the evolution of airliners. The DC-6 and the Lockheed Constellation were selling extremely well and they were pleasing their customers. Boeing's Stratocruiser wasn't doing terribly well, nor were most of the European liners of the era. In England, de Havilland took a chance on the Comet, the world's first jetliner. A series of spectacular Comet crashes convinced much of the world that jetliners weren't safe. Boeing wasn't convinced and started working on a jetliner. Douglas and Lockheed stuck with what worked, and through most of the decade, they remained *very* successful.

In 1953–1954, with the Korean War over and the economy booming, both Douglas and Lockheed each brought out a much improved version of their most successful products: the Douglas DC-7 and the Lockheed Super Constellation. The key to the DC-7 was not that it was really a new aircraft—because the DC-7 had essentially the same airframe as the DC-6—but that it had a really new engine. The DC-7 would be designed around the 3,250-horsepower Wright R 3350 Turbo-compound engine.

The R-3350 was a much more complex engine, and, although it had a good record in military service, it was a Pandora's box of potential field maintenance headaches for the airlines. Nevertheless, it offered greatly improved speed and range, and that's what the airlines wanted. Specifically, they wanted sufficient range to cross the Atlantic Ocean westbound—against the wind—without the obligatory refueling stop in Newfoundland, which cost the flights at least two hours. In the Pacific, the DC-7C now permitted the airlines to bypass Wake Island, which had been a necessary stopover since the days of the Pan American Clippers in the 1930s.

For Douglas, the DC-6 was still in production, but the company's leading airline customers had been operating it for six years, a veritable eternity in the technologically fast-paced 1950s. Through the decade, the United States was in the midst of the greatest burst of prosperity in history. Air travel had become part of everyday life. People who a generation before would have taken the train, now took the plane without a second thought. A vacation in Hawaii or a trip to Europe, which were only recently a once-in-a-lifetime

The first DC-6B in Douglas company markings in flight in December 1952. This aircraft made its maiden flight on February 10, 1951, and became the standard production model of the DC-6 series. It carried 7 percent more passengers than its predecessor, and it was more economical.

event for a handful of people, had become plausible for anyone in the rapidly expanding middle class. With this in mind, the airlines were clamoring for newer and bigger airliners.

It was an era of unprecedented consumerism. Americans bought new cars, new homes, and new appliances for their new homes at a rate that would have been unimaginable to any previous generation. And in these new purchases, the consumers demanded that their new acquisitions should not only be new but look new. Styling became important. For cars, styling changed dramatically for every model year to a degree that had not been seen before and has not been seen since.

In any other decade, Douglas's leading commercial customers might have been happy with a gradually improved DC-6, such as a DC-6C, but in the climate of the times, the DC-7 was not only new, its name sounded new, just as Lockheed's L-1049 Super Constellation would not be just a "new" Constellation, it would be a "Super" Constellation.

As had been the case with the DC-6, it was American Airlines and United Air Lines that launched the DC-7 program. Each airline started with an order of 25 aircraft, and ultimately, deliveries totaled 58 and 57 aircraft, respectively. Eastern Airlines would be a close third with 50 aircraft.

The DC-7 made its maiden flight on May 18, 1953, and the first delivery—to American Airlines— came on November 4. It had the same wing as the DC-4 and DC-6, with a span of 117 feet 6 inches. The length, however, was increased to 108 feet 11 inches— as compared to 93 feet 5 inches on the DC-4 and 100 feet 7 inches for the DC-6, giving the new aircraft a passenger capacity of about 110, depending on configuration. The DC-7 weighed 144,000 pounds fully loaded and fueled and had a service ceiling of 25,000 feet. The four Wright 872TC-18 (R-3350) Turbo-Cyclone engines gave it a cruising speed that was listed at 334 miles per hour but would actually be higher.

The first revenue flight came on November 29, 1953, on American Airlines transcontinental *Mercury* service. When the DC-7 was introduced, the goal had been to cut the coast-to-coast flight time in the United States from the 10 hours required by the DC-6 to under 9. However, on April 4, 1954, an American *Mercury* DC-7 set a transcontinental commercial speed record, having flown from New York to Los Angeles in five hours 51 minutes—at an average speed of 420 miles per hour.

Delta Air Lines, which ordered 10 DC-7s, began service on April 1, 1954, with not one, but three flights, between Chicago and Miami. These were the *Royal Biscayne*, the *Royal Poinciana*, and, finally, the overnight flight, the *Owl Comet*. A year later to the day, Delta began flying DC-7s into the Caribbean.

By this time, Douglas was in the process of having to make some important decisions about the future of its commercial transport business. Since World War II, Douglas had been the world's leading producer of four-engine propliners, with Lockheed providing the only serious competition. However, the successful first flight of Boeing's first jetliner prototype on July 15, 1954, led to cautious steps in that direction. Because jetliner technology was still a new

A Douglas DC-6B in Continental Airlines "Blue Skyway" markings. Continental used DC-6Bs on its Midwest routes but bought only three. They were one of Bristol's main American customers for the British-made Viscount, a DC-6B competitor.

Torkil Viking, the first Douglas DC-6B delivered to the Scandinavian Airlines System (SAS). Eventually, the trinational SAS consortium would buy 31 DC-6s from Douglas, more than any other European customer.

A moody view of the Scandinavian Airlines System (SAS) DC-6B *The Royal Viking* taken in the foggy morning darkness in April 1957. The Scandinavian carrier used the name "Viking" to identify most of the propliners in its fleet. Naming of individual aircraft by airlines was more common in the 1950s than it is today.

LAN-Chile, or Lineas Aereas Nacionales, Chile's national airline, bought seven DC-6B aircraft but did not purchase a DC-7 directly from Douglas.

and uncertain field, Douglas hedged its bets with an ambitious project to enlarge the DC-7.

The "super DC-7," which would be designated DC-7C, was preceded by an interim, improved DC-7 that was designated as DC-7B. The DC-7B made its first flight on April 21, 1955, and flew its first revenue service with Eastern Airlines on May 25. Less than two weeks later, Douglas formally announced that it would begin development of the DC-8 jetliner.

All 50 of Eastern's DC-7s would be of the DC-7B type and nearly half of American's fleet of 58 were DC-6Bs, but all of United's 57 were basic DC-7s. The big three DC-7 customers, American, United, and Eastern, would opt not to buy the DC-7C.

The long-awaited DC-7C made its first flight on December 20, 1955. It was nicknamed "Seven Seas," as much for the pun value of the "7C" designation, as for its 4,600-mile global range, which gave it the capability to fly routes across any of the world's oceans or continents. Indeed, it was Pan American World Airways that first put the Seven Seas to work, beginning service on its sprawling network of routes across the Pacific Rim on April 18, 1956. On June 1, Pan American extended Seven Seas service to its Atlantic routes between the United States and Europe. In February 1957, SAS put the Seven Seas to work on its Polar Route between Copenhagen and Tokyo, and in September, Pan American's DC-7Cs were flying across the North Pole between San Francisco and London.

The biggest customers for the Seven Seas were, of course, the carriers with long, over-water routes. Pan American ordered 25, after having ordered seven DC-7Bs. Another important U.S. carrier with overseas routes, Northwest Airlines, bought 14 DC-7Cs. Koninklijke Luchtvaart Maatschappij (KLM, Royal Dutch Airlines) placed two orders totaling 20 aircraft and SAS bought 18. Both British Overseas Airways (BOAC) and Belgium's Sabena bought ten, while Alitalia bought two, Japan Airlines bought four, Mexicana bought four, and Swissair bought five.

The DC-7C had a wingspan of 127 feet 6 inches, 10 feet greater than the earlier DC-7s, which was accomplished by expanding each wing root by 5 feet. In turn, this placed the especially noisy engines farther from the cabin. The cabin, meanwhile, was lengthened to accommodate more passengers, increasing the overall length to 112 feet 3 inches. The DC-7C weighed 143,000 pounds fully loaded and fueled and had a service ceiling of 21,700 feet. The four Wright R-3350-18EA Turbo-compound engines each had a horsepower rating of 3,400.

Despite the increase in range that was afforded by the R-3350s, it was these engines that illustrated the shortcomings of the Seven Seas. First, they were far more complex and less reliable than earlier piston engines. Second, they *were* piston engines. By 1958 the first Boeing jetliners

were in service, and the airlines recognized their value immediately. They cruised at speeds that were nearly double that of the piston-engine propliners, and they had a greater passenger capacity.

Boeing had been right about jetliners. Had Douglas invested its technical and financial resources on its DC-8 jetliner sooner, it would not have had to play catch-up when Boeing brought out the 707. Nevertheless, 338 aircraft of the DC-7 series were built, including 108 DC-7Cs, all of them in Santa Monica between 1952 and 1958. This represents a rate of better than 56 a year, compared to 64 annually for the DC-6, an aircraft

that is remembered as being much more commercially successful.

By the mid-1960s, none of the original customers for the beautiful DC-7s still had the type in service. In the secondary market, the DC-7 would not fare well. While surplus DC-3s, DC-4s, and DC-6s would still be flying at the end of the twentieth century, the complexities of the R-3350s had grounded most of the remaining DC-7s before the 1970s began. Even the military, which had stepped in to acquire examples of all the other Douglas propliners, was silent. There

were no U.S. military variants of the DC-7, making it the only "DC" aircraft since the one-of-a-kind DC-1 to not have had a military version.

Lockheed, meanwhile, had responded to the DC-7C, not with a jet but with a stretched Constellation, the Model L-1649, which was renamed "Starliner," and with the shorter-range, turboprop-powered Model L-188 Electra. The DC-7C and the Starliner were the ultimate piston-engine propliners, but their days were numbered before they were born. The propliner era was over.

A Douglas DC-7B in the markings of National Airlines. National bought just four DC-7Bs, choosing to wait a short time and begin to convert its fleet to jetliners.

Right
A Douglas DC-7 from the first batch of the type delivered to United Air Lines. Both United and American Airlines bought 25 DC-7s to help Douglas launch the program. United Air Lines would eventually acquire 57 of the aircraft, a total that included no DC-7Cs.

A Douglas DC-7B in the livery of Eastern Airlines, circa early 1960s. After its initial round of DC-7B orders, Eastern eventually brought the total number in its fleet to 50.

The first Douglas DC-7C in company markings, circa 1956. The first flight occurred just before Christmas in 1955, and eventually the aircraft became the ultimate Douglas propliner.

The *Flagship Missouri*, the third Douglas DC-7 delivered to American Airlines. After ordering the first 25 DC-7s, American pushed its total buy to 58, more than anyone else.

The delivery ceremony for the first Douglas DC-7C "Seven Seas" destined for British Overseas Airways (BOAC). Company founder Donald Wills Douglas himself is immediately to the left of the podium with his arms folded.

33

CHAPTER THREE

THE CONSTELLATION:

Lockheed's Lovely Connie

Best known by its nickname, "Connie," the Lockheed Constellation is considered to have been the most elegantly designed of all the great postwar, four-engined propliners, and it was certainly Lockheed's signature propliner.

As with the Douglas DC-4, the idea for the Lockheed Constellation originated before World War II. Like Douglas, Lockheed had previously produced several reasonably successful, small, twin-engine airliners. The Lockheed Model 10 Electra had been operated by airlines from Europe to Australia, throughout Latin America and in the United States by companies from Northwest Airlines to Northeast Airlines. It was also operated by British Airways, one of whose Electras carried Prime Minister Neville Chamberlain to his famous "peace in our time" summit conference with Adolf Hitler in 1938.

The Lockheed Model 10 was also Amelia Earhart's airplane of choice for her ill-starred round-the-world attempt in 1937. The Lockheed Model 14 Super Electra had also been sold to airlines worldwide, and one had been used by playboy industrialist Howard Hughes for his record-setting round-the-world flight in 1938. This was also the beginning of Hughes interest in Lockheed that culminated in his attempts to buy the company in the early 1970s.

As with Douglas, the step to a larger four-engine aircraft was a natural for Lockheed. By 1939, Lockheed had begun development work on its Model 44 (L-044) Excalibur project and was close to finalizing a deal with Pan American World Airways to become the launch customer for the new aircraft. In June 1939, however, Jack Frye, the president of Transcontinental & Western Air (TWA), and Howard Hughes, who was now TWA's largest shareholder, approached Lockheed to discuss their desire for a four-engine, pressurized airliner that would be larger than either the proposed Excalibur or the pressurized Boeing Model 307 Stratoliner. They also wanted an airliner that could fly a transcontinental route without the need to stop for fuel.

Lockheed chief engineer Hall Hibbard and chief aerodynamicist Clarence "Kelly" Johnson went to work on the TWA requirement and created the Model 49 (L-049), which was originally referred to as the Super Excalibur. Johnson, the future head of Lockheed's fabled

The second Lockheed L-049 Constellation to serve with TWA in the airline's natural metal look of the late 1940s. The famous "white top" TWA livery would be introduced for later Connies.

"Skunk Works" Advanced Research Projects Division, was primarily responsible for the design of the Constellation, but Howard Hughes would always insist that he was the true "father" of the aircraft. He felt that it had been his vision of a large, pressurized airliner that had led to its creation, and he would come to resent any claim that anyone else—especially Johnson—had for its genesis.

The Model 49 was designed to accommodate 44 passengers in seats, or 20 in sleeping berths. As was the custom of the time, passenger aircraft had to compete with the Pullman passenger cars on the railroads, which offered berths for passengers traveling long distances.

Like the Douglas DC-4E, but unlike the production DC-4s, the Model 49 had a triple tail. The flowing, nonlinear contours of its fuselage were unique and distinctive, something that would set the Connie apart visually from all other propliners.

Officially renamed as the Constellation before the prototype was built, the Model 49 would have a wingspan of 123 feet and a length of 95 feet 2 inches. It would weigh 86,250 pounds fully loaded and fueled and had a service ceiling of 25,500 feet. It was to have hydraulic controls, as well as full feathering and reversing propellers. To provide customers with a choice, two different radial powerplants were chosen, and it was planned that each of the first two

A Lockheed C-69 Constellation in USAAF markings, circa 1945. Although it was a sturdy and reliable aircraft, the C-69 attracted little interest from the military. The USAAF inherited those ordered by Pan American and TWA but did not go ahead with a dedicated military production version during the war.

TWA flight attendants with one of the airline's Lockheed Constellations. Everything about the Connie was bigger than folks had been used to, including its complement of flight attendants. One or two stewardesses could handle passengers in a DC-3, but a Connie required at least six.

36

A 1944 TWA publicity image of a demonstration of Constellation passenger capacity using the C-69. Clearly the Connie could carry more people than the airliners that folks were used to at the time.

aircraft built would have a different engine choice. The first one was to be powered by four 2,000-horsepower Pratt & Whitney R-2800 Double Wasps, and the second by four 2,000-horsepower Wright R-3350 Double Cyclones. Either engine choice was capable of giving the Model 49 a top speed of 360 miles per hour, better than some of the top fighter aircraft of the era.

In 1940, Hughes and TWA accepted the Lockheed proposal and ordered 40 of the R-3350-powered variant. Pan American quickly passed over the Model 44 that had previously been offered and also ordered 40 Constellations. Hughes permitted Lockheed to sell "his" airliner to another airline when the manufacturer conceded that it would not sell the Connie to another American transcontinental carrier. Pan American was strictly an overseas operator, so that was considered by Hughes to be acceptable. Eastern Airlines, who would later be the only other major domestic operator of Constellations, was

active primarily on north-south routes along the Eastern Seaboard, which generally did not compete directly with TWA.

At the end of 1941, when the United States entered World War II, all production of commercial aircraft was halted. Metal had already been cut for several Model 49 aircraft, but the first of these aircraft was far from being complete. A military acquisition of a promising new aircraft would have seemed to have been a natural choice, but such a move was surprisingly slow to materialize. It was not until September 1942 that the USAAF finally ordered Lockheed to resume production on the Constellation for military use. Under the designation C-69, a total of 22 aircraft from the initial commercial orders were to be built for the USAAF with their interiors each reconfigured to carry 64 passengers.

The first Model 49/C-69 was finished and test flown from Burbank, California, on January 9, 1943, with test pilot Eddie Allen at the controls

The Constellation made the San Francisco-to-Bombay TWA route map shown at the bottom into a reality. For people alive in the 1940s, the notion of flying from San Francisco to Bombay must have seemed nearly like science fiction.

and Kelly Johnson aboard. Allen, on loan to Lockheed from Boeing, was then regarded as the leading test pilot of four-engine aircraft in the United States. He was killed later that year in a crash of the Boeing XB-29.

Since TWA technically owned it until it was officially delivered to the USAAF, the first Model 49/C-69 carried a civilian registration number, although it was painted in USAAF olive drab with USAAF insignia. This first Constellation was formally turned over to the USAAF in July, but because

TWA owned it in in the meanwhile, Howard Hughes took advantage of this fact to show off. He personally piloted the aircraft from California to Washington, D.C., completing the flight in just under seven hours, an exceptional speed for an aircraft of this size. Hughes made sure that the media knew that such an aircraft would be flying TWA's routes as soon as the war was over!

The USAAF eventually ordered 313 Constellations, but most of these would never be built. Because of timing issues and Lockheed's other commitments to the war effort, the USAAF gave a low priority to development of the C-69 and chose instead to make the Douglas C-54 its standard four-engine transport. Nevertheless, the USAAF had explored a number of concepts for production C-69 aircraft during World War II. The C-69A designation was assigned to a Model L-049 variant that would have accommodated 100 troops. The C-69B corresponded to Lockheed's Model L-349 and would have been a troop transport with increased fuel capacity and extended range. The L-249 model number was reserved for a bomber version of the Constellation, which was given the USAAF designation XB-30, but which never got beyond a few preliminary sketches. Late in the war, Lockheed proposed a variant with a thermal de-icing system that was tentatively designated as C-69D but never built. The original L-049 prototype was tested with this system and was temporarily redesignated as XC-69E.

As the war came to a close during the summer of 1945, only 15 of the original 22 C-69s had been delivered. Lockheed was, in turn, released to finish the seven C-69s that were then on the assembly line, as commercial L-049s. They never served in the military for even a moment.

The first commercial Constellation made its maiden flight in TWA livery on August 25, 1945—even before World War II officially ended—and it was turned over to the airline in November. On December 4, this TWA Constellation made a non-passenger demonstration flight to Europe from Washington, D.C. The flight lasted just under 13 hours, with stops in Gander, Newfoundland, and Shannon, Ireland. On February 6, 1946, a TWA L-049 carried its first paying transatlantic customers from New York's LaGuardia Airport to Orly Airport in Paris. TWA began its domestic transcontinental flights nine days later, kicked off with a special flight from Los Angeles to New York—piloted by Howard Hughes himself—that carried a large number of Hollywood celebrities.

British Overseas Airways Corporation (BOAC) was the first European carrier to offer Constellation service across the Atlantic, beginning with a debut on July 1, 1946, between London and New York. The British flag carrier began Constellation operations between London and Montreal on April 15, 1947. Air France was the second European Constellation operator to sell transatlantic tickets for the L-049, beginning its service on February 1, 1947, between Paris and New York with stops in Gander and Shannon.

TWA (now renamed as TransWorld Airlines) remained Lockheed's biggest customer for the basic L-049 Constellation, acquiring a total of 28. Pan American bought 22 and American Overseas Airlines (a division of American Airlines) acquired seven. Among the European carriers, the national flag carrier of the Netherlands, Koninklijke Luchtvaart Maatschappij (KLM, Royal Dutch Airlines), bought six, and both BOAC and Air France ultimately put four into service. Venezuela's Linea Aerea Venezolana (LAV) would buy two.

The second commercial version of the Constellation was the L-649, with the L-149 through L-549 designations having been set aside for the civil and military versions that were not built. There were 14 L-649s, and these were built exclusively for Eastern Airlines. Each was powered by four Wright 749C-18BD engines, the civilian equivalents of the military R-3350 engines. The L-649 Constellation was similar to

A Qantas L-749A Constellation carrying an under-fuselage Speed-Pack to accommodate extra cargo. The Australian flag carrier began service with Connies on its new Sydney to London service in December 1947.

the L-049, but in addition to the different engine type, it offered improved soundproofing and air conditioning, and a gross weight of 94,000 pounds. Development of the L-649 was initiated in May 1945, and the first flight occurred on October 18, 1946. Eventually all of the L-649s would be upgraded to L-749 standard.

The L-749 was essentially an L-649 that was structurally strengthened to accommodate outer wing fuel tanks and a gross weight increased to 102,000 pounds. The L-749A was designed for 107,000 pounds gross, and one L-749 was demonstrated at 133,000 pounds. It retained the same engines as the L-649 and was optimized for long-distance flying. Actually, other engine types, such as the Pratt & Whitney Double Wasp and the Bristol Centaurus, were suggested as options, but only the Wright 749C-18BD was chosen by the customers.

As with the L-049, TWA would be Lockheed's biggest L-749/L-749A customer, with 38 aircraft. Eastern bought seven, Chicago & Southern bought six, and Pan American bought four. Among foreign carriers, KLM led the way with 20. Air France was a close second with 19, followed by Air India with 7, South African Airways with 4, Aer Lingus with 5, Qantas and South African with 4 each, Avianca with 2, and Aerovias Guest with 1.

Qantas' Constellation acquisition was the first step in an ambitious plan by the Australian government to turn the former regional carrier into a world-class international airline. Qantas, originally the Queensland & Northern Territory Air Service, had evolved into Qantas Empire Airways, which served as the eastern link of BOAC's London to Australia route until June 1947, when the Australian government bought out the BOAC interest and started replacing its converted Lancaster bombers with Constellations. The first Qantas through service from Sydney to London was operated with a Constellation on December 1, 1947. This inaugurated what was, at first, a weekly service. It would not be until May 1955, however, before Qantas had regular Constellation service between Australia and Tokyo.

The L-749 also attracted the attention of the U.S. military. The USAAF—a reluctant customer for the C-69—became the independent U.S. Air Force in 1947, and soon after, the service began taking a second look at the Constellation.

To symbolize a fresh interest in the Constellation, the C-69 designation was scrapped and supplanted by the designation C-121. In 1948 ten L-749s were ordered as C-121A personnel transports and one was ordered as VIP executive transports under the designation VC-121B. Three of the C-121As also became VC-121A executive transports. One of these was assigned to General Douglas MacArthur, the Supreme Allied Commander in the Pacific, and one to General Dwight Eisenhower, the Supreme Allied Commander in Europe. General MacArthur named

his VC-121 *Bataan*, after the peninsula in the Philippines where American troops under his command had fought heroically against the Japanese invaders in 1942. General Eisenhower named his Constellation *Columbine*, after the state flower of Colorado, his wife's home state.

The VC-121B was earmarked for use as a presidential transport, but it was reassigned to "Special Air Missions" because President Harry Truman preferred to use a Douglas VC-118, which he had

The original Lockheed L-049 Constellation prototype as modified in 1950 to serve as the L-1049 Super Constellation prototype. The wily Howard Hughes sold it back to the manufacturer for ten times what he'd paid for it.

Military and civilian L-1049 Super Constellations on Lockheed's Burbank, California, delivery ramp. The late 1950s were an exciting time at Burbank. Employment was at its highest peacetime level and the order books were full. There were 117 and 135 Super Connie airframes delivered in 1955 and 1956.

A Lockheed L-1049 Super Constellation in the livery of Eastern Airlines, circa 1952. Eastern Airlines was the first carrier to operate a Super Connie, using it on December 7, 1951, between New York and Miami. Eastern would buy 40 Super Connies from Lockheed.

nicknamed *Independence* after his home town in Missouri. The VC-121B differed from the VC-121As in that it had a longer range and an especially deluxe interior. Eventually the three VC-121As and three C-121As were brought up to VC-121B standard. After Eisenhower was elected president in 1952, one of these became his presidential aircraft and was given the name *Columbine II*. This aircraft was, in turn, replaced by a VC-121E (L-1049B) named *Columbine III*. It was during Eisenhower's administration that the radio call sign "Air Force One" became the standard

name for any U.S. Air Force aircraft with the president of the United States aboard, regardless of type.

In the late forties, the U.S. Navy also became a customer for the L-749. The requirement was not for a transport but for a long-range patrol aircraft capable of supporting a large radar system. Douglas proposed the DC-6, but the triple-tail configuration of the L-749 proved to be more aerodynamically compatible with the large radome, and two were ordered in 1948 under the designation PO-1W (Patrol, Lockheed), which would be changed to WV-1 (Airborne Early Warning, Lockheed) in

1952, two years after the second of the two aircraft was delivered.

Lockheed considered a marriage of the L-749 airframe with the Wright Turbo-Cyclone engine under different configurations that would have been designated as L-849 or L-949, but the company abandoned this idea in favor of an enlarged airframe aircraft that would be designated as L-1049 and known as the "Super" Constellation.

The prototype of the L-1049 Super Constellation series was actually the original L-049 prototype, which Lockheed bought back from Howard Hughes in 1950. Because this original aircraft had been built with an unpressurized fuselage, it was not considered by the USAAF to be worth hanging on to, so it was declared as surplus after the war and sold to Hughes for $10,000. When Robert Gross, the chairman of the board of Lockheed, went to Hughes personally to make the deal to get it back, Hughes quoted him a price of $100,000 for the aircraft. Gross reluctantly agreed because both men knew that it would cost Lockheed more than that to build a new, enlarged Constellation from the ground up.

A classic view of a Lockheed L-1049 Super Constellation in TWA markings, with the New York City skyline in the background. The "look" of the Super Connie so completely defined the identity of TWA in the late 1950s that the carrier was later than its competitors in making the switch from propliners to jetliners.

Dutch maids tidy up an L-1049 Super Constellation in Koninklijke Luchtvaart Maatschappij (KLM, Royal Dutch Airlines) markings at Lockheed's Burbank, California, facility. It was the sort of corny photo-op that made for a guaranteed placement in newspapers on slow news days.

Lockheed cut the 049-1961 fuselage in two places, and inserted extension segments fore and aft of the wing, lengthening the fuselage from 95 feet 2 inches to 113 feet 7 seven inches. Initially, straight sections were inserted, but they did not blend well with the flowing, porpoise-like lines of the Connie. The original fuselage was not a straight tube, so the straight inserts had to be reworked so that the handsome lines of the original configuration would be retained in the longer L-1049. The prototype actually made ten test flights with the straight inserts before the empennage was

modified. During these flights, it was discovered that the deeper forward section had a destabilizing directional influence, as the original vertical tail surfaces were not of sufficient area. Consequently, Lockheed engineers had to increase the height of the outboard vertical surfaces by 18 inches to achieve directional stiffness. Lockheed also incorporated Hughes' idea of providing more headroom for the pilot.

The Super Connie's fuselage extension permitted greater fuel capacity and an increase in seating capacity from 69 to 92 in an all-economy-class configuration.

The L-1049 cabin had rectangular windows rather than the circular portholes of the earlier Connies. The gross weight was increased to 120,000 pounds, but the wingspan remained unchanged at 123 feet.

The powerplants initially chosen for the L-1049 production series were 18-cylinder Wright 956C-18CA Double Cyclones, although the prototype flew for the first time on October 13, 1950, with Wright 749C-18BDs.

The production L-1049 was first flown on July 14, 1951, and within 90 days, Lockheed had received over $100 million in orders. The Super Constellation first entered service with Eastern Airlines on December 7, 1951, between New York and Miami. In October 1953, TWA would inaugurate nonstop Super Constellation service from Los Angeles to New York. Lockheed eventually built 14 L-1049s for Eastern and 10 for TWA. The Eastern Super Connies were configured for 88 passengers, while TWA's carried 75 on domestic routes or 65—with sleeping arrangements—on long overseas flights. When the performance of the basic L-1049 turned out to be inferior to the Douglas DC-6B, however, Lockheed went back to the drawing board for an improved version.

The L-1049C would be the second commercial Super Constellation, with both the L-1049A and L-1049B having been military variants. Meanwhile, Douglas had also returned to its own drawing board to create its new DC-7. The Wright 872TC-18DA Turbo-Cyclone, a turbo compound engine in the R-3350 family that provided more power with less fuel consumption than the Double Cyclone, was selected for both the Lockheed L-1049C and the competing Douglas DC-7.

A Turbo-Cyclone engine had first been installed in 049-1961 for testing back in late 1951, and the three power-recovery turbines brought a step up in performance. The exhaust gas would drive the three turbines, and these would, in turn, drive the crankshaft. When Lockheed planned the Model 1049C, the engines were intended to fly at altitude with the compressor operating at the high blower setting. In 1951, however, this engine, with three power-recovery turbines feeding power to the engine crankshaft, Wright had not adequately flight tested it at high altitude. It did have several years of testing on the Lockheed P2V Navy patrol aircraft, but this had been at altitudes of 10,000 feet or lower. Six times in a row during the 1951 flights, a fire occurred on one of the turbines when the test aircraft reached 16,000 feet. It became evident that if this problem was not found and fixed, there could be no L-1049C.

The solution to the problem involved designing a new cooling cap, which was essentially a static radiator placed over each turbine wheel. The original cap had the cooling air pickup at the center of the turbine wheel. The centrally located outlet on the cooling cap was connected to a tube that would aspirate the cooling air through the exhaust pipe. There were six exhaust cylinders exhausting through one tailpipe, and the exhaust gas from each of the six cylinders would drive the turbine wheel and, in turn, would put energy into the engine crankshaft. There were round holes on the inboard side of each blade. There was a fluid coupling between the turbine wheel and the crankshaft, with a seal between them, and this, being the lowest of the three power-recovery turbines, would leak oil and catch fire. With the redesigned cooling cap, however, the air from the holes on the rotating turbine wheel were picked up and radiated over the cooling holes, and the radiator ejected the hot air tangentially.

The Turbo-Cyclone-powered L-1049C made its debut on February 17, 1953, three months ahead of the rival DC-7. Lockheed would deliver the aircraft at a rate of four per month for a year, beginning in June. Eastern was the biggest customer, ordering 16, and Air France and KLM were close with 10 and 9, respectively. Trans-Canada bought five and Air

The first-class interior of the Lockheed L-1049 Super Constellation. While first-class interiors in modern jetliners are pretty nice, they don't compare to the Pullman-like comfort aboard a Super Connie.

India took two. Qantas and Pakistan International each ordered three.

Because of the Super Constellation's greater range, Qantas was able to cut 20 hours off the flight time on its route between Sydney and London by eliminating the necessity for an overnight stop in Singapore. This faster service was inaugurated on March 2, 1956, and two years later, in January 1958, Qantas would use a Super Constellation to begin regularly scheduled around-the-world service via London. The westbound service was designated as the *Southern Zephyr*, while the eastbound route was the *Southern Aurora*.

A convertible passenger/freighter version of the L-1049C, with reinforced floors and main-deck cargo doors, was produced as the L-1049D. Four of these were built for Seaboard & Western Airlines.

By the middle 1950s, the American automobile industry had adopted the practice of rolling out an entirely new car for each model year. This car would be built for a year and then generally replaced by a newly redesigned model. New model cars had always been designated for the coming year to accentuate their newness, but in the 1950s, the automakers went to great lengths to make each new model appear distinct from the previous year's model. For about four years during this period, Lockheed became caught up in this marketing concept, and was doing the same with Constellations. The L-1049C/L-1049D was the "1954 Connie," the L-1049E was the "1955 Connie," the L-1049G would be the "1956 Connie," and the last Super Constellation, the L-1049H, would fill the bill for 1957.

The L-1049E offered an increased gross weight—up to 135,400 pounds for takeoff—for seven customers who took delivery between May 1954 and April 1955. Qantas ordered nine and KLM bought four. Air India, Avianca, Iberia, and Trans-Canada each bought three, while LAV and Cubana bought two and one, respectively.

Making its debut on December 7, 1954, the L-1049G was to be the definitive Super Constellation. Indeed, 40 percent of all Super Connies were of the variant that was marketed simply as the "Super G." The L-1049G entered service with Northwest Airlines on July 1, 1955, the first of four for that carrier. The Super G was similar to the L-1049E, but, once again, the gross takeoff weight increased, this time to 140,000 pounds. There was an engine change as well. The Super G would be delivered with four Wright 972TC-18DA-3 Turbo-Cyclones, each offering 3,400 horsepower.

Lockheed's original customer for the Constellation family, TWA, was the leading customer for the Super G, buying 28. Meanwhile, Howard Hughes, TWA's biggest shareholder, bought one for himself through his Hughes Tool Company. Air France bought 14 L-1049Gs, and Eastern, the penultimate American Super Connie operator, added 10 to its fleet. Among the other major world flag carriers, Lufthansa took eight; KLM and Brazil's Varig bought six each; Trans-Canada bought four; Cubana, Thai Airways, and Transportes Aereos Portugueses (TAP) each bought three; Iberia, LAV, and Qantas added a pair to each of their fleets; and Avianca acquired one.

The L-1049H bore a relationship to the L-1049G that was similar to the relationship of the L-1049D to the L-1049C. It had all of the "Super G" improvements and enhancements, but, like the L-1049D, it had the beefed-up floor structure that allowed it to serve as a cargo carrier. Actually, it was originally marketed as being convertible between a passenger and/or a freighter configuration. Because of this, the largest L-1049H customer was the all-freight airline, Flying Tigers, who bought 13 of the 53 that were sold. Both Seaboard & Western and California Eastern bought five, and National Airlines, Aerovias Real, and TWA bought four each. Air Finance Corporation, Slick Airways, and KLM each took three, while Qantas, Resort Airlines, Pakistan International, and TCA each bought two. Dollar Airlines, an affiliate of Robert Dollar's San Francisco-based steamship company, bought a single L-1049H from Lockheed.

Unlike the situation with the early Constellations, the U.S. Air Force and the U.S. Navy were the leading customers for the L-1049 *Super* Constellation, buying over half of those built. The U.S. Air Force continued the "C-121" designation series begun with the L-749, and ordered 33 L-1049Fs as C-121C personnel transports and 10 as RC-121C airborne early warning aircraft, with the "R" implying a reconnaissance role. The U.S. Navy ordered 65 L-1049Bs as personnel transports under the designation R7V-1 (originally R7O-1 before Lockheed's naval designation letter changed to "V"), but 10 of these were diverted to the U.S. Air Force as C-121Cs and one went to the Air Force as President Eisenhower's VC-121E, *Columbine III*. This aircraft would be the last presidential Constellation. After his election in 1960, John F. Kennedy briefly used a Douglas VC-118 before converting to a Boeing 707 jetliner procured under the U.S. Air Force designation VC-137.

The Lockheed L-1649 Starliner (foreground), which entered service in 1957, was clearly much larger than the L-1049 Super Constellation. It was the obvious next step in the evolution of the Connie, and had it not been for the advent of jetliners, it would have been a historic milestone and not merely a footnote.

The U.S. Navy also ordered 224 L-1049As as airborne early warning aircraft under the designation WV-2. Although 22 of these were subsequently cancelled, this represented the largest order for a single Constellation or Super Connie variant ever. Of the 202 total built, 124 (still the largest order) were actually delivered to the Navy, with the remainder being diverted to the U.S. Air Force under the designation RC-121D. The RC-121C and RC-121D were very similar to one another except for the wingtip fuel tanks on the RC-121D.

The radar equipment and internal systems on the RC-121C and the RC-121D were also similar, but these evolved over time as missions changed and as technical upgrades became available. After 1962, when Navy designations merged with those of the U.S. Air Force, the WV-2s were redesignated as EC-121K, EC-121L, or EC-121M, depending on their specific mission. The "E" prefix reflected their use in electronic countermeasures and related operations. At the same time, the U.S. Air Force RC-121Cs and RC-121Ds were also redesignated as EC-121C and EC-121D because the "E" more accurately represented their use than did the "R." Some Navy EC-121Ks were later redesignated as EC-121Ps when equipped for antisubmarine operations.

The airborne early warning and electronic warfare Super Constellations were given the military name "Warning Star" (the "star" theme being nearly always present in the naming of Lockheed aircraft), but they were generally referred to as "Connies." An exception would come when they were deployed to Southeast Asia during the Vietnam War era of the late 1960s and early 1970s. During this period, they were identified with the code names of their specific missions.

In Southeast Asia, some U.S. Air Force EC-121Ds were upgraded to serve as Airborne Warning And Control System (AWACS) aircraft, and were redesignated as EC-121Q. These had operated in this role for the Air (later Aerospace) Defense Command (ADC) under the code name "Big Eye," but after March 1967, the EC-121Qs in Southeast Asia became known as "College Eye."

At the same time, 30 former Navy EC-121K and EC-121P aircraft were reassigned to the U.S. Air Force in Southeast Asia to monitor the Project Igloo White electric sensors that had been installed along the Ho Chi Minh Trail and to coordinate attacks against such targets. These aircraft had their large radomes removed, and were known as EC-121R "Batcats."

During the development of the Super Constellation, Lockheed considered the potential next steps in Constellation evolution. One fork of the evolutionary path would include a turboprop-powered Constellation, while the other would include a Constellation that would be still larger than the Super Constellation. The former was examined under the model designations L-1149 and L-1249. The L-1149 would have been essentially identical to the L-1049G, but powered by four Allison 501D2 turboprop engines.

While the L-1149 was never built, four of the L-1249s came to life as the U.S. Navy R7V-2 and the U.S. Air Force YC-121F (two each), which were used in testing the Pratt & Whitney YT34-P-12A turboprop engine. The first of these carried the name *Elation*. Technically, these were built under the designation

FLY TWA
TRANS WORLD AIRLINES
Super Constellations
Litho. in U.S.A.

A Lockheed L-1649 Starliner in the livery of Lufthansa, circa 1957. Germany's flag carrier was one of two European airlines to buy the Starliner, but it did so merely as an interim step while waiting for its first jetliners.

L-1249A to distinguish them from the version that Lockheed planned to market commercially under the designation L-1249B. Ultimately, the L-1249B was never built as Lockheed moved toward development of the Electra, a new four-engine turbo-prop airliner.

As for an enlarged "Super" Super Constellation scenario, Lockheed first considered adopting the process that had been used in 1950 to create the Super Constellation. This would have involved inserting fuselage-lengthening extensions in the Super Constellation, just as the Super Constellation had been created by "stretching" the original Constellation configuration. Under this scenario, the Model L-1449 design called for a 55-inch extension, while the L-1549 would have been 95 inches longer than the L-1049. However, neither of these was to be built, as Lockheed engineers decided in 1954 to completely scale up the entire aircraft, including the wings, as well as the fuselage.

This new aircraft would be designated L-1649 and named "Starliner" to distinguish it from the Constellations. Why Lockheed wanted to move away from one of its best-loved trade names is one of those mysteries of marketing that has never been fully explained. The L-1649 Starliner's overall appearance was distinctly that of a Constellation, though, and it was usually referred to in the field as a Constellation.

The L-1649 was 109 inches longer than the L-1049G, enough to accommodate nearly 100 passengers, but the big change was in the size of its wing. The span of the new L-1649 wing was 150 feet, compared to 123 feet 5 inches in the L-1049G, and the wing area was increased from 1,654 square feet to 1,850 square feet. For passengers, the good news was that the engines were over 5 feet farther from the cabin, thus reducing noise considerably. For power, Lockheed considered turboprop engines, but settled on Wright 988TC-18EA-2 Turbo Cyclone turbo-compound radials.

TWA announced an order for 25 L-1649s in 1955, and the first Starliner made its maiden flight on October 10, 1956. It entered service with TWA between New York and Paris on June 1, 1957, and on the 19-hour, nonstop haul between Los Angeles and London on September 30.

While the L-1649 is arguably the best and most beautiful propliner that ever flew, its timing placed its debut at the dawn of the jet age and at the threshold of its own obsolescence. Within 18 months of its entering service, the Starliner was competing on the North Atlantic route with jetliners that could carry half again more passengers in half the time. Nevertheless, Air France ordered 10 and Lufthansa ordered 5 to tide them over until they could get their first jets into service. An additional four that had been ordered by Linee Aeree Italiane were diverted to TWA when LAI became a subsidiary of Alitalia.

There was no military version of the Starliner, although the U.S. Navy assigned the designation W2V to a possible airborne early warning version that was never produced.

In the late fifties, airliner technology was evolving more rapidly than it ever had. The introduction of jets revolutionized the field. If it had been introduced in 1955, the L-1649 would have reigned supreme. However, within three years of its introduction, the L-1649 was essentially obsolete. During the early sixties, the major airlines stopped using propliners on their primary routes, and many Starliners, like their Constellation sisters, were converted for freight use or sold to second-tier airlines.

For Eastern Airlines, the Constellation/Super Constellation fleet would provide the means to begin offering its low-cost "shuttle" service on the Eastern Seaboard. When it began in April 1961, the Eastern Shuttle linked Boston, New York, and Washington with eight daily flights costing $12 between Boston's Logan Airport and New York's LaGuardia Airport, and $14 between New York and Washington National Airport. Super Constellations would serve on this route until 1968.

Among the second-tier carriers that began flying with secondhand Constellations in the early sixties was Air Afrique, which was founded in 1961 by 12 French-speaking African nations to begin service between Paris and west African hubs in Cameroon and the Ivory Coast.

Constellations would continue to operate on passenger routes until the late seventies and in air freight service until the late eighties. A handful of flight-worthy Constellations were still operating at the turn of the century.

CHAPTER FOUR

THE STRATOCRUISER:

Boeing's Last Propliner

The Model 377 Stratocruiser was the only four-piston-engine commercial transport aircraft developed after World War II by the airframe builder that, during the war, had become the world leader in the design and production of four-engine aircraft. It was the sister ship of the largely identical Model 367 Stratofreighter military transport that went into service with the U.S. Air Force under the C-97/KC-97 family of designations. Both aircraft types were based on the revolutionary Model 117 wing that Boeing produced during World War II for the ultra-long-range B-29 (Model 345) Superfortress strategic bomber, which was probably the most advanced large aircraft to go into production before 1946.

Historically, the Model 367/377 family served during the era between the greatest wartime achievement in large airplane technology—the Boeing B-29—and the foundation of the greatest dynasty of commercial aircraft in aviation history—the Boeing "700 series" jetliners. Indeed, the Model 367/377 program would climax with the 367-80, the prototype for the Model 707 jetliner. This program was to be the cornerstone of the "700 series" jetliners that have been ubiquitous on the world's airways for half a century.

The Model 377 Stratocruiser would be Boeing's last piston-engine airliner, while the Model 367 KC-97 Stratofreighter was the first aircraft dedicated to aerial refueling to go into routine squadron service.

Overall, the airframes for both the Model 367 and Model 377 were generally the same, with the different model numbers used mainly to distinguish the military from the civilian end user. The differences were primarily in avionics, interior layout, and the addition of clamshell doors and/or refueling gear on the Model 367.

The original troop carrier idea—which had blossomed during the critical year of 1944 as the U.S. military was moving millions of men throughout the world—faded with the end of World War II, so Boeing moved ahead with plans to market the commercial Model 377 variant of the big aircraft to the airlines under the name "Stratocruiser." The implication was that the aircraft, with its pressurized cabin, would cruise in the stratosphere, high above the nuisance of weather.

The Model 377 Stratocruiser would ultimately have a decade of service with a half dozen first-tier airlines—and longer with second-tier users—where it earned high marks with crews for its spacious flight deck, and with passengers for its comfortable cabin and luxurious lower deck salon.

The first Boeing Model 377 Stratocruiser in Boeing markings in flight in March 1948. Owned by Pan American World Airways, this ship joined Pan American's fleet as *Clipper Nightingale* after being used for an extensive series of flight tests.

total of 888 Model 367s. The Model 367, mainly under the KC-97F and KC-97G designations, would serve longer and in larger numbers with the U.S. Air Force and the Air National Guard than the Model 377 did with any airline.

The roots of the Model 367/Model 377 program can be traced to the concept of adapting elements of a four-engine bomber for commercial use—which, for Boeing, began in the late thirties, when it created the Model 307 Stratoliner, using the wing of the B-17 heavy bomber. The Stratoliner was the first Boeing aircraft named with the "Strato" prefix that Boeing favored for many years, and the first airliner with a pressurized cabin to go into service in the United States. First flown in 1938, the Model 307 might have proven itself to be a worthy competitor to the remarkable Douglas DC-3, but World War II intervened and the evolution of commercial aviation lay dormant until 1945. Only ten Model 307s were built, and only

A Northwest Airlines Boeing Model 377 Stratocruiser in flight near Washington's Mount Rainier. It was standard operating procedure at Boeing to photograph its new aircraft over the perpetually snow-capped summit of Washington's highest peak.

In its Stratocruiser advertising, Northwest Airlines stressed the stratospheric altitude and the ability to fly above the weather. While Pan American pioneered North Atlantic routes with its Stratocruisers, Northwest looked toward the Far East.

The Stratocruiser had a wingspan of 141 feet 3 inches, 1 foot greater than the B-29, and it was 110 feet 4 inches long, compared to the B-29's 99 feet. Wing area was 1,720 square feet, compared to 1,739 for the B-29. The gross weight was 135,000 pounds, although that would later increase to 148,000 pounds. The top speed was 375 miles per hour and the cruising speed was 340 miles per hour at a cruising altitude of 25,000 feet. The service ceiling was 32,000 feet and the range was in excess of 4,200 miles.

The engines were four Pratt & Whitney R-4360 Wasp Majors, which delivered 3,500 horsepower on take-off, compared to the 2,200 horsepower of the B-29's Wright R-3350 Twin Cyclones.

In the late forties, after a lapse in interest of several years, the U.S. Air Force revisited the Model 367, and—after the delivery of 64 commercial Stratocruisers—Boeing would fill Air Force orders for a

eight went into airline service—three with Pan American and five with Transcontinental & Western Air (TWA), the precursor of TransWorld Airlines (TWA).

During the war, Boeing engineering genius George Schairer created the Model 117 wing, which gave the B-29 Superfortress a range that was unprecedented for bombers and which permitted the U.S. Army Air Forces (USAAF) to conduct a strategic offensive against Japan in 1944 and early 1945 that would not have been possible using any other aircraft type.

Even as the B-29 was inching toward its first flight in 1942, Boeing president Philip Johnson instructed its developers to begin thinking about a transport version that could be marketed to the USAAF immediately and possibly to commercial customers after the war had ended. Chief engineer Edward Wells and Wellwood Beall, the vice president in charge of engineering, began tentative work on engineering studies directed toward a transport based on the Model 345/B-29.

Drawings for the Model 367, laid out in a troop carrier configuration, were completed over the summer and submitted to General Oliver Echols at the Air Materiel Command at Wright Field. The wing was the same, of course, but the fuselage was a pair of pressurized cylinders that gave the Model 367 its distinctive "figure eight" cross-section. The bottom of the two cylinders had roughly the same dimensions as the B-29's fuselage, and it was designed to be used as a cargo hold. Overlapping it by several feet, the larger upper cylinder was designed to ultimately accommodate up to 134 soldiers and their gear—or 40 to 55 people in large comfortable first-class seats.

Another aspect of troop transportation that was of growing interest to the USAAF by the end of 1942 was that of casualty evacuation. By the end of the war, it would become a matter of policy to use aircraft in all cases where critical patients needed to be evacuated to the U.S. mainland, but as early as 1942, the USAAF was beginning to lay the groundwork for this capability. With this in mind, Beall and his team designed the Model 367 to carry 83 stretchers.

On January 23, 1943, the USAAF placed its initial Model 367 order. Three of the aircraft were ordered under the designation XC-97, but the project was not placed on the same fast track as the B-29 had been. Despite the fact that the pressurized XC-97 was larger than the unpressurized Douglas C-54, the latter would remain as the primary four-engine USAAF transport for the duration of the war simply because

it was already in production and it could be produced quickly in the required numbers. Boeing could promise a great deal with the XC-97, but the company couldn't promise the rapid rate of production that Douglas was already delivering.

The first XC-97 flight occurred on November 15, 1944, and early in 1945, the USAAF ordered 10 YC-97 service test aircraft. When the war ended a few months later, the military project was put on a slow track, and the first YC-97 flight did not take place until March 11, 1947. However, with the war now over, commercial airlines were anxious to resume a full level of service with the best aircraft available, and Boeing was able to unveil the commercial version of its Model 367, the Model 377 Stratocruiser.

In 1945, America's international flag carrier, Pan American World Airways placed the first order for Stratocruisers, a total of 20, valued at $24 million. During the early months of 1946, additional airlines also began to announce orders for the Model 377. On February 28, 1946, Svensk Interkontinental Lufttrafic (Swedish Intercontinental Airlines, SILA) announced the purchase of four Stratocruisers to establish a 14-hour New York to Stockholm non-stop service. Subsequently, SILA would enter into a

The lower deck lounge in the Boeing Model 377 Stratocruiser was a pleasant place to sit and relax on a long flight. However, the ceiling was too low for tall people to stand comfortably, and publicity photos were usually not taken with tall people actually standing.

The original Boeing Model 377 Stratocruiser in flight over Mount Rainier during early testing, circa July 1947. Actually, the flight this day was probably more of a photo-op, as Boeing liked to pose its aircraft against the backdrop of the picturesque volcano.

partnership with airlines in Denmark and Norway to form the Scandinavian Airlines System (SAS), a multinational carrier serving all three countries.

Northwest Airlines became the first U.S. domestic carrier to buy the Stratocruiser, announcing on March 13, 1946, the signing of a contract involving $15 million for the purchase of a fleet of ten of the big airliners. The Stratocruiser was seen by Northwest as means to provide seven-hour, coast-to-coast, non-stop service.

One week after the Northwest announcement, Harold Harris, vice president and general manager of American Overseas Airlines, the overseas division of American Airlines, said that his airline would acquire eight Stratocruisers for service on the North Atlantic. The Model 377's range would permit non-stop flights between New York and London and other European destinations.

On August 30, 1946, Lord Winster, Britain's Minister for Civil Aviation, announced that the British Overseas Airways Corporation (BOAC) would become the second non-American customer for the Stratocruiser. BOAC would put six of the aircraft into service on its Atlantic Speedbird routes. This order represented the second purchase of Boeing aircraft by BOAC, the first being the purchase in 1941 of the now famous three Model 314A flying boats, the *Bristol*, *Berwick*, and *Bangor*, which combined to accumulate a total of 596 Atlantic crossings during World War II. The *Berwick* was used frequently by Prime Minister Winston Churchill.

The first of a total of 56 Model 377s made its debut flight on July 8, 1947 in Boeing markings under the civil registration number NX90700. This aircraft was the only Model 377-10-19. The other Pan American aircraft would be designated as Model

377-10-26s. Each would have 61 main deck seats and 25 seats when the aircraft were configured with sleeping berths.

After being used as a flight test aircraft, NX90700 would be upgraded to 377-10-26 standard and repainted. It was delivered to Pan American in 1950, having been re-registered as N1022V and named *Clipper Nightingale*. The second Stratocruiser, the first 377-10-26, made its first flight on September 29, 1947, painted in Pan American markings as *Clipper Good Hope*. *Clipper Golden Gate* made its first flight in Pan American markings on April 17, 1948, followed by *Clipper Bald Eagle* on October 7. Initial deliveries would be delayed considerably by a four-month strike that occurred at Boeing's Seattle plant during 1948.

The first four Stratocruisers were used in flight testing, so the fifth Model 377, *Clipper America*, was actually the first to be delivered to Pan American. This first delivery occurred on January 31, 1949, and *Clipper America* began service between San Francisco and Honolulu—the airline's busiest route—on April 1. The number four Model 377, *Clipper Bald Eagle*, joined Pan American on March 14, and on June 1, the airline announced its "President" all-first-class service between New York and London using Stratocruisers.

All but nine of the 56 Stratocruisers were delivered to the airlines during 1949, and four of the remaining nine would be delivered in January 1950. The first non-Pan American Model 377s were delivered in June 1949. These were *Flagship Great Britain*, delivered to American Overseas on June 13, and two Northwest aircraft, *Stratocruiser Minneapolis-St. Paul*

One of the two Pan American World Airways Boeing Model 377 Stratocruisers to wear the name *Clipper America* is seen here over San Francisco Bay, with Alcatraz and the Bay Bridge clearly visible below and in the background.

Pan American's Boeing 377 Stratocruiser *Clipper Monarch of the Skies*, which was originally the American Overseas Airways *Flagship Norway*. When Pan American took over the former American Overseas equipment, they gave them "Clipper" names ending in "of the Skies."

The British Overseas Airways (BOAC) Boeing Model 377 Stratocruiser *Caledonia* in natural metal finish as it was originally delivered. This ship was the third of its kind to be delivered to the British flag carrier, and one of five delivered during 1949.

Flight attendants prepare for meal service in the galley of a Boeing Model 377 Stratocruiser. The galley aboard the Stratocruiser was among the first in an airliner to approximate the future industry standard.

and *Stratocruiser Chicago*, both of which were delivered on June 22. The American Overseas aircraft were designated as Model 377-10-29 and were essentially the same as Pan American's 377-10-26s. The Northwest aircraft were designated as 377-10-30 and were equipped with an APS-42 weather radome such as was installed in the military C-97A. The 377-10-30 seated 61 in the main cabin or 28 when 16 sleeping berths were made up. The 377-10-30 was also distinguished from other models by its rectangular windows rather than the round "portholes" of previous Stratocruisers.

Pan American's twelfth Stratocruiser, *Clipper Seven Seas*, was delivered on the same day as the first two Northwest aircraft, marking June 22 as the biggest day of deliveries during the program. On September 28, United Air Lines received *Mainliner Hawaii*, the first of seven that the carrier acquired for use on its routes between Hawaii and the West Coast of the mainland United States. The United Stratocruisers were designated as 377-10-34 and were the only aircraft other than the Northwest 377-10-32s to have rectangular windows. They seated 56 on the main deck, or 20 when 17 berths were made up.

The first BOAC Stratocruiser, *Cathay*, was delivered on October 12, by which time the British carrier had become Boeing's only foreign

Stratocruiser customer. During the spring, SAS had decided to withdraw from the program with its first three aircraft nearing completion and already registered (one each in the three nations of the international consortium). On May 10, after several rounds of negotiations, Boeing agreed to transfer the four SAS contracts to BOAC. This brought to ten the number of Stratocruisers under construction for the British "Speedbird" fleet. The first of the former SAS aircraft was delivered to BOAC on October 24 under the name *Champion*, and all of the SAS aircraft were delivered by the end of the year. The SAS Stratocruisers were designated as Model 377-10-28 and had seating for 55 on the main deck or 20 when 17 berths were made up. They also had a private stateroom aft and a luxury compartment in the front. The Stratocruisers of the original BOAC order were designated as Model 377-10-32 and had seating for 60 on the main deck or 20 when 17 berths were made up.

An indication of the high regard in which the Stratocruiser was held came in October 1949. BOAC chose to use the Stratocruiser *Canopus*, rather than a British-made aircraft, to carry Princess Elizabeth (later

Queen Elizabeth II) and her husband, Prince Philip, across the North Atlantic on a state visit to Canada.

The final Northwest Model 377, *Stratocruiser Orient Express*, was delivered on December 21, and the last Pan American aircraft was delivered nine days later. The last American Overseas Stratocruiser, *Flagship Scotland*, was turned over on January 5, 1950, marking the first delivery of the new year. United's last Stratocruiser, *Mainliner Kano*, was delivered on January 28. The only deliveries in February and March were the final four of BOAC's original order. For Boeing, the Stratocruiser production program officially came to a close on March 24, 1950, with the delivery of *Castor* to BOAC, although the actual last delivery came on October 24 when the original prototype was turned over to Pan American after three years of flight testing.

Before the end of 1950, American Overseas was absorbed by Pan American and its Model 377-10-29s joined the 377-10-26s in Pan American's fleet.

Flagship Great Britain became Pan American's *Clipper America*, *Flagship Holland* became *Clipper Sovereign of the Skies*, *Flagship Ireland* became *Clipper Romance of the Skies*, *Flagship Sweden* became *Clipper Queen of the Skies*, *Flagship Denmark* became *Clipper Good Hope*, and *Flagship Scotland* became *Clipper Eclipse*.

By April 3, 1950, a week after the delivery of the last Stratocruiser to be built, the fleet had already carried 160,000 passengers more than nine million miles. Over the course of the next six years, the Stratocruisers would transport 4.1 million passengers and log more than 250 million miles. This would include 18,400 Atlantic crossings and 15,500 transpacific flights.

For most of its first six years, the Stratocruiser represented the leading edge of luxury air travel. The Model 377 aircraft all offered an extra wide passenger cabin and mirrored his-and-hers dressing rooms. In a sleeper configuration, the Stratocruiser was equipped

The Pan American World Airways Boeing Model 377 *Clipper Constitution* makes a stop in Honolulu in June 1950, nine months after it entered service with the airline. Hawaii was an essential stopover point for all the Clippers on Pan American's transpacific route.

59

with upper-and-lower bunk units equipped with heavy curtains for privacy.

A circular staircase led to the lower-deck lounge, which was comfortably appointed like the club car on a passenger train. This lounge served as the social center for passengers on the long, intercontinental flights. People could read or play cards, drinks and snacks were served, and United even experimented with the installation of a television set.

Flight attendants prepared hot meals in what was a state-of-the-art galley. With the largest galley (350 cubic feet) ever installed in a commercial airplane, stewards had facilities to turn out as many as 24 complete meals in 18 minutes. Meals prepared from frozen or refrigerated food would be served by all the airlines that operated Stratocruisers. Put aboard through a special service door, the precooked and frozen food was kept in dry ice containers, then heated at meal time in two electric ovens. Seven two-gallon containers—each with its outlet and individual switch for heating and built-in dry ice container for cooling—supplied the juices, soups, and drinking water for the trip. A five-gallon urn was installed to permit fresh coffee to be brewed in flight. Common today, this system was seen as a major innovation in the late 1940s.

Perishables other than those included in regular precooked frozen meals were stored in a water ice refrigerator at the aft end of the galley. Its capacity was 17 cubic feet, three times the size of most airline refrigerators at the time. With weight-saving construction throughout, the galley was entirely aluminum with the exception of three stainless-steel working surfaces.

BOAC would be the first airline to reconfigure some of its Stratocruisers with economy seating. The all-first-class Stratocruisers were typically configured to carry 55–61 passengers, but they often carried fewer than 40. In 1953, Northwest modified most of its fleet to carry 83 tourist-class passengers in more closely spaced seating with minimal legroom. A year later, BOAC followed suit, modifying eight of its aircraft to seat 81.

The luxurious ambiance afforded by the Stratocruiser was soon offset by a growing reputation for unreliability. Constantly recurring problems with the Pratt & Whitney R-4360 Wasp Majors caused numerous delays, and there were many cases where Stratocruisers had to turn back from long transatlantic or transpacific flights because of engine trouble. It became hard for the airlines to tout the joy of traveling abroad in a plush new Stratocruiser if passengers had to carry the nagging fear of turning back as an alternative to having to "ditch" in the icy waters of the North Atlantic.

During the first four full years of service, three Stratocruisers were lost in crashes. The first was United's *Mainliner Oahu*, which crashed into San Francisco Bay during a training flight on September 12, 1951. All three crewmembers aboard were killed, but the aircraft was carrying no passengers. The first crash with loss of passengers came on April 29, 1952, when Pan American's *Clipper Good Hope* crashed into the Brazilian jungle on a flight from Buenos Aires to New York. All 50 people aboard were killed when the

number two engine separated from the aircraft and the highly unbalanced Stratocruiser became uncontrollable. On July 24, 1954, BOAC's *Cathay* crashed at the airport at Prestwick, Scotland, killing 28 of the 36 people on board. This time, the cause was pilot error.

Between 1955 and 1957, four well-publicized Stratocruiser crashes in the Pacific marked the public relations turning point for the aircraft. In three of these, engine or propeller failure was to blame, and in one case, the Stratocruiser disappeared without a trace. On March 26, 1955, Pan American's *Clipper United States* went down on a flight between Portland, Oregon, and Honolulu when the number three engine wrenched off the aircraft due

to a faulty propeller. All but four people survived to be rescued, and as a result, the CAA mandated Stratocruiser hollow steel propeller blades be replaced with solid metal blades. On April 2, 1956, Northwest's *Stratocruiser Tokyo* ditched in Puget Sound on a flight from Portland to Seattle, with the loss of five. On October 16 of the same year, Pan American's *Clipper Sovereign of the Skies* was on the Honolulu to San Francisco leg of an around-the-world flight from Philadelphia to San Francisco when its number four engine failed and the propeller could not be feathered. The pilot was able to ditch the aircraft in mid-Pacific with no loss of life. Passengers were not so lucky a year later when Pan American's

Passengers disembarking from a United Air Lines Boeing Model 377 Stratocruiser. These well-dressed travelers seem to be going nowhere, but actually they were part of a demonstration held at Boeing Field in 1949 aimed at showing how many people could be accommodated in a Stratocruiser.

61

Clipper Romance of the Skies simply vanished in roughly the same area on November 9, 1957, with 44 on board.

During the 1958–1959 period, as Stratocruisers were rapidly being phased out in favor of jetliners, three Pan American Stratocruisers were lost in crash landings. *Clipper Golden Gate* was lost on June 2, 1958, at Manila; *Clipper Seven Seas* crash-landed on April 10, 1959, at Juneau; and *Clipper Australia* made a belly landing in Tokyo on July 9, 1959. The only loss of life was a single fatality in the Manila crash.

While there were 56 commercial Model 377s, the U.S. Air Force bought 888 military Model 367s. After three XC-97s, ordered in 1942, there were six YC-97s, three YC-97As, and a YC-97B ordered in 1945. All of these were delivered in cargo/troop carrier configuration, and one was used during the Berlin Airlift of 1948–1949. The one YC-97B became the one C-97B,

The American Overseas Airlines Boeing Model 377 Stratocruiser *Flagship Great Britain* became one of the two Stratocruisers to fly for Pan American under the name *Clipper America* when the latter airline absorbed the former.

The wide-aisled Boeing Model 377 Stratocruiser. The thick pile carpet is evident and it is hard to believe that this is not a Pullman car. Seating was typically four-abreast, although Stratocruisers were variously configured with single or double aisles.

which later became one of three VC-97Ds that were used by the Strategic Air Command as flying command posts.

Subsequent U.S. Air Force deliveries included 50 C-97As and 14 C-97Cs, ordered in 1948 and 1950, respectively, which were cargo/troop transport aircraft with "clam-shell"-type rear cargo doors.

By 1950, with the beginning of the Korean War and the growing concern about the Cold War, the United States armed services underwent a dramatic buildup on a scale unprecedented since World War II. For the U.S. Air Force, this would involve an expansion of long-range bomber operations within the Strategic Air Command. To extend the range of the bombers then in service, the U.S. Air Force developed a practical means of inflight refueling and set out to procure an aircraft dedicated to serve as an aerial refueling tanker. The aircraft chosen was the C-97. In 1951 the U.S. Air Force ordered 60 refueling aircraft under the designation KC-97E and another 159 as KC-97F. All of these were theoretically convertible to the transport role but with their clam-shell rear cargo doors sealed.

The 592 KC-97Gs ordered from 1951 through 1953 were true dual-role military aerial refueling aircraft that had accommodations for 96 troops or 69 stretchers on the top deck without the need for removing the refueling tanks that were located on the lower deck. In order that the KC-97Gs could keep up with faster jets, 82 of them were fitted with a pair of J47-GE-25A turbojets to supplement the power of their piston engines. These aircraft were redesignated as KC-97Ls.

The C-97s were assigned primarily to the Military Air Transport Service, with whom they flew numerous casualty evacuation missions during the Korean War, flying critically wounded patients from staging areas in Japan to hospitals in Hawaii or the mainland United States. The KC-97 fleet served initially with the Strategic Air Command, but as the Boeing KC-135 Stratotanker jet refueling aircraft entered service in the late 1950s, the KC-97s were gradually withdrawn to other commands and to the Air National Guard, with whom they would serve until the 1980s.

During the Vietnam War, the U.S. Air Force KC-135 fleet was concentrated in Southeast Asia, so the KC-97s took up the slack for the U.S. Air Force in Europe and other areas throughout the world.

The only other major military operator of the 367/377 series was Israel, which used former commercial Model 377s rather than Model 367s. In 1962 the Israeli Defense Force Air Force acquired five to begin forming a heavy lift capability to replace its fleet of French Nord Noratleses and Douglas C-47s and DC-3s. Among these were the former Pan American *Clipper America* and *Clipper Southern Cross*. Eventually, the Israeli Model 377s were replaced by the Lockheed C-130 Hercules, but one of them remains on static display as the sole surviving Stratocruiser.

After the Pan American takeover of the American Overseas fleet during the first year of commercial Stratocruiser operations, the next mass shift in Stratocruiser ownership came in 1954, when United Air Lines sold its entire fleet to BOAC. *Mainliner Hawaii* became *Cleopatra*, *Mainliner Kauai* became *Coriolanus*, *Mainliner Hana Maui* became *Cordelia*, *Mainliner Waipahu* became *Cameronian*, *Mainliner Hilo* became *Calypso*, and *Mainliner Kano* became BOAC's *Clio*.

The Stratocruisers remained in first line service with Pan American, Northwest, and BOAC through most of the 1950s. Eventually, though, as the jet age approached, they were sold off to secondary operators as the major airlines moved to jetliners.

The Stratocruiser's career as a passenger carrier with its original first-tier airline operators ended at 8:35 on the evening of September 15, 1960, when the last Northwest Stratocruiser touched down in Minneapolis-St. Paul after a flight from New York. Over the course of a decade, the Northwest Stratocruiser fleet had carried 3,732,309 passengers 70,495,022 miles. Although an era had ended, many of the surviving Stratocruisers would have another decade or more of service with smaller, second-tier airlines.

Probably the most important secondary operator of Model 377 Stratocruisers was Transocean Airlines, which operated them between Hawaii and the West Coast of the United States during the 1950s and 1960s. Just as BOAC had picked up the ex-United Air Lines Stratocruisers in 1954, the British carrier sold most of its fleet to Transocean in 1958 and 1959 as it upgraded to jetliners. *Champion, Caledonia, Centaurus, Cassiopia, Caribou, Cambria, Canopus, Cabot,* and *Castor* all joined Transocean. Four of these were modified to carry 117 tourists in high-density configuration, while the others were retrofitted to carry up to 96.

Among those that served with Pan American, *Clipper Bald Eagle, Clipper Trade Wind, Clipper Flying Cloud, Clipper Golden Eagle, Clipper Mayflower, Clipper Flying Eagle, Clipper Fleetwings, Clipper*

A United Air Lines Boeing Model 377 Mainliner during her delivery flight in August 1949. United took delivery of four Stratocruisers during 1949 and had them in service in time to take vacationers to Hawaii for the Christmas holidays.

The Aero Space Lines "Guppy" and "Super Guppy" conversions of Boeing 377 Stratocruiser airframes resulted in the aircraft with the greatest interior volume ever.

Constitution, *Clipper Invincible*, and *Clipper Morning Star* were all traded in to Boeing for credit toward the purchase of a Model 707 jetliner in 1960 or 1961. Lockheed also received its share of trade-ins in 1959 when Northwest decided to exchange its Stratocruiser fleet for L-188 Electras. *Stratocruiser Minneapolis-St. Paul*, *Stratocruiser Washington*, *Stratocruiser Alaska*, and *Stratocruiser Orient Express* were traded in to Lockheed in 1959, and *Stratocruiser New York* followed in 1963.

Most of these were, in turn, sold for scrap, but several, like their former BOAC sisters, were resold to second-tier passenger airlines, such as Linea Internacional Aerea and Rutas Aereas Nacionales SA (RANSA) of Venezuela, which turned six Stratocruisers into cargo carriers.

Nine Stratocruisers went to Aero Space Lines, which rebuilt them as large cargo carriers by tripling their internal volume to 22,500 cubic feet. These were known as the "Guppy" transports because they took on the appearance of huge pregnant fish when their cargo holds were ballooned. The first was called the "Pregnant Guppy," and it

was followed by five larger "Super Guppies" and three smaller "Mini Guppies." The latter were smaller than the Super Guppies, but slightly larger than the original Pregnant Guppy.

The Model 377 was 110 feet 4 inches long, while the Pregnant Guppy was 127 feet long; the Super Guppy was 141 feet 3 inches long; and the Mini Guppy was 132 feet 10 inches long. The empty weight of the Model 377 was 78,930 pounds, while the Pregnant Guppy's weight was 91,000 pounds; the Super Guppy's was 108,000 pounds; and the Mini Guppy's was 90,000 pounds.

The Guppy fleet was originally developed to serve the NASA manned space program, especially the Apollo lunar landing project, which was active during the 1960s. Because the program required time-critical delivery of numerous enormous components, the Guppies were a vital link in keeping the project on schedule.

After the end of the Apollo program, the Guppies served customers around the world for another two decades. Ironically, Boeing's major commercial competitor, Europe's Airbus Industrie, used Guppies extensively through the 1980s.

CHAPTER FIVE

THE CONVAIRLINERS:

Sturdy Short-Haul Workhorses

A great deal of emphasis is often placed on the grand four-engine propliners of the post-war era, but there was still a need for shorter-range, twin-engine aircraft to operate in more densely populated areas such as northern Europe, the Northeastern United States, and California. The Douglas DC-3 had been the ideal aircraft for such a purpose in the mid-1930s, but a decade later, technology had advanced and it was time for a change. Douglas made a stab at addressing the need with its Super DC-3, but, for the most part, the Southern California planemaker focused its attention and its resources on the DC-4 and DC-6.

Perhaps the most important twin-engine airliner to be developed in the United States in the late 1940s was the product of a San Diego-based manufacturer that had built the four-engine aircraft, which was produced in the largest numbers during World War II. The Consolidated Vultee Corporation was formed in 1943 by the merger of Consolidated Aircraft Corporation and what was then the Vultee component of the Aviation Corporation (AVCO). Consolidated Vultee was known as "Convair" almost immediately, but the name was not officially registered until the entity became the Convair Division of General Dynamics Corporation in 1954.

During the war, 18,482 examples of the Convair B-24 Liberator strategic bomber were produced, primarily for the USAAF and Britain's Royal Air Force, and another 774 of the similar PB4Y Privateer were built, mainly for the U.S. Navy.

As World War II was winding down, Convair considered a commercial airliner version of the B-24 and actually built two "Liberator Liners." Also under consideration was an airliner based on the gargantuan, six-engine XC-99 military transport, which was itself derived from the B-36 intercontinental bomber, the largest combat aircraft ever built. However, both of these commercial projects would be shelved.

As Douglas, Lockheed, and Boeing were moving ahead with their four-engine transports, Convair turned its attention to a family of twin-engine propliners. This series of aircraft, known collectively by the name "Convairliner," became one of the company's most successful postwar programs, and certainly its most successful nonmilitary program ever.

Ivar Viking, the Scandinavian Airlines System (SAS) Model 440-75 Metropolitan on the San Diego assembly line. SAS was the third commercial customer for the Metropolitan.

Convair executives and a grim-faced Philippine Airlines flight crew commemorate the first Model 340 Convairliner delivery to the carrier.

A Pan American Model 240-2 Convairliner buzzes Lindbergh Field as a Western Air Lines Model 240-1 prepares for takeoff. By January 1949, Western had received its final aircraft and Pan American's deliveries were almost complete.

ever flown, even including the later aircraft in the series. In September 1947, after just 14 months of flight testing, the Model 110 was deemed unnecessary and unceremoniously cut up for scrap.

By the time of its first flight, the unpressurized Model 110 was clearly seen as a mere prototype for a bigger (slightly) and better (certainly in terms of performance) production series. By the end of 1945, the pent-up demand by first-tier airlines for new equipment resulted in a shower of orders. For American Airlines, this would mean the need to rebuild service on its vast network of short domestic routes, and for Convair, this would mean an order for 100 pressurized aircraft in the same general size and weight class as the Model 110.

The first production Convairliner was the Model 240, which took its designation not from the sequence of Convair model numbers, but from the idea marketing description, "2 engines, 40 passengers."

The American order for 100 Model 240s was soon augmented by orders from Continental Airlines, Koninklijke Luchtvaart Maatschappij (KLM, Royal

The idea was to create a short-range airliner with postwar technology that could replace the venerable DC-3 on domestic—as well as overseas—feeder routes. Convair management realized that American society was going to be more prosperous than before the war. People would want to travel, they would want to travel by air, and they would want to travel in aircraft more modern than the Douglas DC-3, which had so completely dominated the prewar airliner market.

The mother ship of the Convairliner series was the one-of-a-kind Model 110, which was conceived in early 1945 before World War II ended, and first flown on July 8, 1946, less than a year after the end of the war. It had a wingspan of 89 feet, and a wing area of 813 square feet. It was 71 feet long with a tail height of 25 feet 2.5 inches. It weighed 35,970 pounds fully loaded and fueled and had a cruising speed of 260 miles per hour at 16,000 feet. It was powered by a pair of 2,100-horsepower, air-cooled, 18-cylinder Pratt & Whitney R-2800-SC13G Double Wasp engines that gave it a top speed of 314 miles per hour. It was configured to accommodate 30 passengers, slightly more than a DC-3 in typical configuration, and it had a range of 560 miles. Company test pilot Sam Shannon later remarked that it was the best aircraft that he had

Dutch Airlines), Pan American, Trans-Australia Airlines, and Western Air Lines, which put 150 Convairliners on the order books before the first Model 240 made its debut at San Diego's Lindbergh Field.

The prototype made its first flight on March 16, 1947, and deliveries to American Airlines began 11 months later on February 23, 1948, although the aircraft did not enter service until June 1.

The initial delivery schedule rotated between three customers. Of the first eight delivered, five went to American, two to Western, and one to Pan American. Generally, this pattern repeated over and over through the first 70 deliveries, with an additional airline added to the cycle beginning with the 32nd aircraft being delivered to Trans-Australian.

The Model 240 Convairliner had a wingspan of 91 feet 9 inches, and a wing area of 817 square feet. It was 74 feet 8 inches long and it had a tail height of 26 feet 11 inches. Its initial gross weight was 40,500 pounds, but this later increased to 42,500 pounds. The Model 240 was powered by a pair of air-cooled, 2,400-horsepower, 18-cylinder Pratt & Whitney Double Wasp engines, either the R-2800-CA3, the R-2800-CA15, the R-2800-CA18, the R-2800-CB3, or the R-2800-CB16.

The 40 seats in the Model 240s' pressurized cabins were arranged in a ten-row, four-abreast configuration. The windows were rectangular, rather than circular "portholes" as had been the case with the Model 110.

All of the Model 240s were generally the same, except for minor interior variations as requested by the customers. For this reason, submodel numbers were used to identify specific types by customers. For example, the Western Convairliners were Model 240-1, the Pan American ones were Model 240-2, the KLM ones were Model 240-4, Trans-Australia received Model 240-5s, and so on. The American Airlines aircraft were designated as Model 240-0, except the final four, which were Model 240-26.

When Model 240 deliveries began, they proceeded quickly. By the autumn of 1948, as Aerolineas Argentinas, KLM, and Trans-Australia put them into service, the Convairliners were flying on four continents. In January 1949, after just 11 months of production, the 100th Convairliner was completed. By this time, Western had received its final aircraft and Pan American's deliveries were almost complete, but American would continue to receive aircraft through the life of the manufacturing cycle, which would continue into 1950.

Additional European airlines using the Convairliner included Swissair and Belgium's Sabena, while in the United States, Northeast Airlines, Central Air Transport, and Continental Airlines all became customers. Late in the program, the Convairliner service area expanded to six continents with sales to Ethiopian Airlines and Garuda Indonesian Airlines. Several private individuals, including Jorge Pasquel in Mexico and Harold Vanderbilt in the United States, acquired the Model 240 as executive aircraft.

The biggest customer for the Model 240 Convairliner, however, was the U.S. Air Force. Of the total of 566 Model 240s that were built, 176 went to civilian customers, 2 were retained by Convair, and the rest were sold to the Air Force as T-29 Flying Classroom trainers or as C-131 Samaritan aeromedical transports. The U.S. Air Force began placing their orders in 1949 based initially on their growing need for multi-engine trainers for bombardiers and navigators. At that time, they were still using converted, leftover World War II bombers, mainly B-25Js, that were getting long in the tooth.

The initial Air Force Convairliner, designated XT-29 (Model 240-17), was first flown on September 22, 1949, and was followed by a second XT-29 and 46 T-29As. These were delivered between March 1950 and October 1951 and were all company Model 240-17. The T-29As were equipped with Pratt & Whitney R-2800-77 or R-2800-97 engines delivering 2,400 horsepower. They were

A Model 340-48 Convairliner in the "De Vliegende Hollander" ("Flying Dutchman") livery of Koninklijke Luchtvaart Maatschappij (KLM, Royal Dutch Airlines).

The Model 340 Convairliner offered the technology by which airlines could provide their customers with speed and efficiency. Compared to what was still in people's recent memory, these features were a true selling point.

similar to commercial 240s, except that they were not pressurized, and they were equipped with various antennas and a large radome on the underside of the fuselage. Inside, they were built with workstations for 14 bombardier or navigator students.

The second batch of U.S. Air Force Model 240s, 105 T-29Bs, were delivered between April 1952 and August 1953. Built as Model 240-27, these were similar to the T-29As, but they were pressurized. They were equipped with the same R-2800-97 engine as the later T-29As. All were used as trainers except for four that were converted to executive transport configuration prior to delivery, and ten that were later loaned to the U.S. Navy.

The T-29B was followed by the virtually identical T-29C (also Model 240-27), of which 119 were delivered between January 1954 and August 1955. The major difference would be the R-2800-99W powerplant. This series also included a couple of personnel transport conversions. Three were loaned to the U.S. Navy in the 1970s and ten were converted for use by the Federal Aviation Administration.

The T-29D (Model 240-52) was originally built as a dedicated bombardier trainer. A total of 92 were delivered between September 1953 and April 1955 as the U.S. Air Force was rapidly expanding its B-47 bomber force. Eventually, at least half were modified as VT-29D executive transports, and during the Vietnam War, 11 were used to train electronic countermeasures teams under the designation ET-29D.

The success of the reliable Model 240 airframe led to the U.S. Air Force's decision to acquire it as the C-131A (240-53) Samaritan, which was essentially a "flying hospital" in the sense that the T-29 had been a "flying classroom." Using the same R-2800-99W as the T-29C and T-29D, the C-131A could accommodate 20 stretchers plus seven seats, or could be fitted with 39

seats. There were 26 C-131As delivered between April and December 1954.

On the commercial side, the Model 240 Convairliner had been a success for Convair, easily outselling the competing Marin 2-0-2, but when Martin introduced its pressurized 4-0-4, the playing field changed. With this in mind, the company developed a fresh new Convairliner, which would be designated as Model 340 and which was announced in November 1950.

First flown on October 5, 1951, the Model 340 was similar to the 240 but was lengthened to accommodate another row of four seats and it offered improved high-altitude capability thanks to better engines and a larger wing. It was certificated with a gross weight of 47,000 pounds, and it was powered by the 2,500-horsepower R-2800-99W engine that was used on the later military Model 240s.

AIRLINES

Air Chief Nanticoke

U.S. carriers that bought a large number of Model 340s included Hawaiian Airlines (as 340-36), National Airlines (as 340-47), and Delta Air Lines (as 340-38).

By the mid-1950s, the European economy had recovered significantly from World War II, and European carriers led a foreign sales slate that was proportionally stronger for the Model 340 than it had been for the Model 240. KLM was a repeat customer of 340-48s, and it was joined by Germany's new Lufthansa (as 340-68), Finland's Finnair (as 340-40), and Italy's Alitalia, which took some 340-41s that were originally ordered by Northeast in the United States. Other foreign sales included 340-42s for Philippine Airlines, 340-49s for Garuda Indonesian, 340-51s for Aeronaves de Mexico, and 340-59s for Brazil's Cruzeiro do Sul.

When Lufthansa began operations with its Convair 340s in April 1955, it was the first time in ten years that German-owned aircraft in German markings had operated in German air space. Under the terms of Germany's surrender at the end of World War II, the former Reich had been forbidden to operate either a national airline or an air force. In 1955, when full sovereignty was restored to the Federal Republic of Germany (West Germany), the new nation was permitted to have both. The new Lufthansa was a successor to the old Deutsche Luft Hansa, which had been Germany's national flag carrier before the war. Parenthetically, the new Lufthansa would operate throughout Germany

A Model 340 Convairliner in the markings of *Air Chief Nanticoke* of Mohawk Airlines. The New York regional carrier named its aircraft after Native American chiefs of its namesake tribe.

The first Model 340 Convairliner shown in comparison to a Douglas C-47, the military version of the airliner (the DC-3) that the Convairliners replaced. In terms of speed and passenger capacity, the Convairliners were truly the "next generation."

United Air Lines was the customer that helped launch the Model 340, taking the first aircraft of the new series on March 27, 1952, four days after it was certified. United received 7 of the first 8 and 19 of the first three dozen. A second strong customer was Braniff International Airways, which was second only to United in the early days of the program.

As with the Model 240s, the Model 340s were generally identical to one another, except for cabin interior changes as requested by the customers. Again, submodel numbers were used to identify specific types by customers. The sequence picked up where the 240 numbers left off, so the prototype was 340-30, the United aircraft were designated as 340-31 and Braniff's were 340-32.

Neither American nor Western joined the Model 340 program, but Continental and Pan American, both earlier Model 240 customers, did buy a few, under the designations 340-35 and 340-54, respectively. Other

and the world for 35 years before it was allowed to operate flights into Berlin. By then, the fleet of Convair 340s would be a distant memory.

The Model 340 also turned out to be a popular corporate aircraft, especially for oil companies for use in oil exploration activities. The oil companies owning them included Aramco (as 340-33), Texaco (as 340-34), and Union Oil of California (as 340-63). Other companies ranged from the American Can Company (as 340-42B) to Union Carbide (as 340-68A).

The total number of commercial sales for the Model 240 had been 176, but Convair would sell 209 commercial Model 340s. Meanwhile, as with the Model 240, there was a military interest in the Model 340 Convairliner. The U.S. Air Force would order 65 under a continuation of the C-131 lineage and the U.S. Navy bought 37 under the designation R4Y-1. The military Convairliners were ordered as convertible transports and used for a wide range of tasks from carrying personnel to airborne testing of electronics and other systems.

The first Air Force 340s were the 36 C-131B (340-70) that were delivered between December 1954 and September 1955 and powered by R-2800-103W engines. These were followed by two YC-131Cs (340-36 and 340-64) that were used in testing the Allison YT56-A-3 turboprop engine. The remainder of the U.S. Air Force 340s were C-131Ds (340-67 and 340-79). Delivered between August 1954 and April 1955, these were used by the MATS as personnel transports. Of these, 16 were delivered as VC-131D with VIP interiors.

The U.S. Navy's R4D-1 (340-71) fleet was delivered with 44 passenger seats like the MATS aircraft, but in service, various numbers of seats were pulled out or moved and other equipment installed for testing or training purposes. The last one, a 340-66 designated as R4Y-1Z had a "plushed-up" executive interior with 24 seats and 6 sleeping berths. The R4Y-1s that were still around after 1962 were redesignated as VC-131F.

Four years after the announcement of the Model 340, Convair announced the introduction of its successor, an aircraft that offered improved performance as well as extra soundproofing, which was an important factor in the competitive field of airliner development as all the manufacturers worked to eliminate noise. Originally referred to as the Model 340B, the new aircraft was soon designated as the Model 440 and was officially given the name "Metropolitan." Like the Model 340, it accommodated 11 rows of passengers sitting four abreast, but a more cramped, 52-passenger arrangement was also available.

The Model 440 Metropolitan had a wingspan of 105 feet 4 inches and a wing area of 920 square feet, 113 percent that of the Model 240. It was 79 feet 2 inches long and it had a tail height of 28 feet 2 inches. Its gross weight was 49,700 pounds, and it had a cruising speed of 299 miles per hour at 13,000 feet. The Model 440 was powered by a pair of air-cooled, 18-cylinder Pratt & Whitney Double Wasp engines, either the R-2800-CB16, rated at 2,400 horsepower, or the R-2800-CB17, rated at 2,500 horsepower. The noise of the engine was decreased by replacing the twin, circular engine exhausts with a single, rectangular exhaust.

The Metropolitan prototype, designated as 440-77, which first flew on October 6, 1955, was followed by the first production aircraft on December 16. Unlike the case of previous Convairliners, when commercial orders had taken precedence over military deliveries, three of the first four Model 440s were military aircraft. The first was a 440-78 for the Royal Australian Air Force and the other two were a pair of an eventual six 440-79s that would be delivered to the U.S. Air Force as C-131Ds. The initial commercial customer to get an airliner was Continental, which put its first 440-35 into service on March 8, 1956.

There was no single major customer for the Metropolitan as American had been for the 240 and United for the 340. In the United States, National, Delta, and Braniff joined Continental in ordering a few, and there were

The well-appointed lounge area of the Model 340 Convairliner operated by Phillips Petroleum featured a television set. In the early 1950s, an airborne television set was a true novelty, and it probably offered poor reception under most conditions.

some large orders from abroad. Swissair took 11 440-11s, Sabena took 11 440-12s, and Brazil's REAL bought 17 440-62s, although three of these were diverted to corporate customers in the United States—General Motors and Hughes Tool Company. A Model 440-0 designation was created to apply generically to aircraft delivered to a number of smaller customers. Canadair, Cruzeiro do Sul, General Motors, Germany's Condor, and Spain's Iberia each took delivery of "generic" 440-0s.

The most well-publicized sale was that of a 440-86 to the Brooklyn Dodgers baseball team. When the team moved west to Los Angeles in 1958, having the airplane was an essential means of integrating the team into the season's schedule, since all but one of the National League baseball teams that the Dodgers played were across the continent. Ironically, the major league team that "replaced" the Dodgers for New York fans was given the same name as the Model 440—the "Metropolitans," better known as the "Mets." In a sense, it can be said that the new team was named for the airplane that took the old team away, though this is almost certainly not what the owners of the Mets had in mind.

In addition to a pair of 440-78s for the Royal Australian Air Force, military customers for the Metropolitan included Germany's Luftwaffe, which bought two 440-0s and the Italian Air Force bought one 440-96. Having acquired six 440-79s as C-131D personnel transports for the MATS, the U.S. Air Force bought 15 440-72s under the designation C-131E. Most of these were used as electronic countermeasures trainers by the Strategic Air Command, but four were used by the

A Model 340 Convairliner of the ramp at Lindbergh Field in San Diego. This was a busy ramp in the early to mid-1950s, and nobody could predict that it would all be over by the mid-1960s.

Federal Aviation Administration for use in monitoring airways. Several of the Strategic Air Command C-131Es were later used for reconnaissance and electronic countermeasures work and were redesignated as RC-131E or EC-131E. The U.S. Navy acquired two 440-71s for transport and training purposes under the designation R4Y-2, which became C-131G in 1962. Orders from the Navy for an additional 33 Model 440s of various types were cancelled. Several other air forces, especially in Latin America, have used Convairliners, but these were acquired secondhand from other customers, mainly airlines, and not directly from the manufacturer.

The last U.S. Air Force C-131E was delivered in November 1957 and the two R4Y-2s followed in January 1958. By the middle of 1958, the last Model 440 was completed, bringing the total of all Convairliner types to 1,076. This made it the third most successful program in Convair history after the PBY Catalina and the B-24 Liberator, both of which were World War II-era military programs.

A next logical step for Convair would have been to create a turboprop-powered successor to the Met-

ropolitan, because the Convairliner airframe had been designed from the beginning with that possibility in mind. However, by 1958, the company was deeply immersed in its Model 880 jetliner program, and jetliners seemed to be the way to the future.

While there would be no production series of *new* turboprop Convairliners initiated by Convair,

The first Model 340-32 Convairliner for Braniff International Airways. The carrier was the second, after United Air Lines, to receive a Model 340.

The first of several Model 440-72s delivered to the U.S. Civil Aeronautics Administration (CAA).

there were a large number of turbo-prop *conversion* projects that would extend well beyond the scope and lifetime of the original production program. The history of Convair-liner turboprop conversions began almost at the beginning of the history of the Convairliner, when Convair experimentally replaced the R-2800 piston engines of the original Model 240 prototype with a pair of Allison 501-A4 turbo-props. Redesignated as the 240-21 and called "TurboLiner," this air-craft was first flown under turbo-prop power on December 29, 1950, making it probably the first commercial turboprop ever flown in the United States. The TurboLiner project was aban-doned and no production air-craft was ever built.

In 1954 the U.S. Air Force converted two Model 340s to turbine power under the desig-nation YC-131C, but this experiment, like Convair's four years earlier, did not lead to a widescale conversion project.

This 1954 magazine ad for the Convair-liner was actually a celebration of all *American* propliners of the era. It showed the foremost such aircraft from each of the top five purveyors of com-mercial aircraft.

Left

The first Model 440-97 Metropolitan delivered to Australia's Ansett Airways. Founded in 1936 by Reginald Ansett, the airline traditionally favored American, rather than British, equipment.

Far Left

A Model 440-12 Metropolitan in the markings of Societe Anonym Belge d'Exploitation de la Navigation Aerienne (Sabena), Belgium's national flag carrier.

A Model 440-62 Metropolitan in the markings of Brazil's Redes Estaduais Aereas Limitada (REAL). The carrier ceased to exist in 1961, when it was absorbed into national flag carrier Viacao do Rio Grande (Varig).

Two years later, Napier & Son in Britain converted one Model 340 and one Model 440 to turboprop power by fitting them with 3,060-engine-shaft-horsepower (eshp) Napier N.El.1 Eland turboprops. The first flight of an Eland-powered Convairliner took place on February 4, 1956, and the aircraft subsequently achieved a speed of 314 miles per hour at 16,000 feet. There was a great deal of interest in the "Convair 540 Cosmopolitan," as Napier called its creation, but there were no orders. One of the aircraft was, however, leased to Allegheny Airlines in the United States in 1959.

The 540 Cosmopolitan attracted a great deal of attention, including the notice of the parent company of Convair itself. General Dynamics was suddenly quite interested in the next logical step in Convairliner evolution—even if Convair was preoccupied with the 880 and did not have the time and resources to take that step. All of the tooling for Convairliner production, which was now lying dormant on the factory floor in San Diego, was ordered to be shipped to Canada to another General Dynamics subsidiary—Canadair.

The idea was that Canadair would resume building new 440 airframes, which would be fitted with Napier Eland engines. These would then be marketed, not as the "Convair 540," but as the "Canadair CL-66A."

The tooling was shipped as planned, but no commercial CL-66As were ever built. However, between July 1960 and March 1961, Canadair did manufacture ten 440-72-type aircraft with Napier Elands for the Royal Canadian Air Force under the designation CL-66B. These aircraft, which were referred to as Cosmopolitans, were designated as CC-109 by the Royal Canadian Air Force. Canadair also re-engined three San Diego-built Model 440 airframes with Napier Elands, and these were designated as CL-66C. Two of these aircraft entered service with Quebecair in 1960.

A Model 440-88 Metropolitan in the livery of Germany's Lufthansa. While Lufthansa bought four Metropolitans, Germany's air force, the Luftwaffe, also acquired the type.

The pilot offers a thumbs up from the cockpit of a Swissair Model 440-11 Metropolitan. One of the early users of the Model 240 Convairliner, Swissair also took delivery of a dozen Metropolitans.

A family pauses to be photographed prior to departing on a Swissair Model 440-11 Metropolitan. Actually, the photographer and the family are all posing for this publicity photograph designed to show the joys of air travel, circa mid-1950s.

The Convairliner turboprop conversion that was produced in the largest numbers was the variant known unofficially as the "Convair 580." In 1957 the Allison division of General Motors—makers of aircraft engines—obtained a YC-131C turboprop conversion from the U.S. Air Force, and retrofitted it with its 501-D13 turboprop engines. In what was known originally as the Allison Prop-Jet Convair project, Allison re-engined 170 Convairliners. In 1964, Frontier Airlines became the first airline to put the aircraft into service, and it was the first to use the unofficial "Convair 580" designation. The type was delivered to more than a half dozen airlines and a large number of independent users.

In 1965, Convair introduced its own turboprop conversions, which were officially known as "Dart Convairs" after the Rolls-Royce Dart 452-4-4K engines that were used. By this time, Napier had been absorbed by Rolls-Royce, which was evolving into Britain's largest aircraft engine maker. Originally the conversions were designated as 240D, 340D, and 440D, with the "D" for

Left

In June 1957, the president of Eastern Airlines—World War I "ace of aces" Eddie Rickenbacker—took delivery of the thousandth Convairliner, a Model 440-86.

Above

A Model 340-23 Convairliner in the markings of Garuda Indonesian Airways. Garuda was formed in 1949 as the state airline of the newly formed state of Indonesia with the help of the state airline of the former colonial power, KLM, Royal Dutch Airlines.

Below

The first Model 600 Convairliner taking off from San Diego's Lindbergh Field in 1965. A total of 38 240s underwent turboprop conversions to become Model 600s.

Dart, but for marketing reasons, and to make the aircraft appear new, the 38 240s converted were redesignated as Convair 600s, and 27 340s and 440s became Convair 640s. The 440s that became 640s were also known as "Super Metropolitans."

Central Airlines put the first Model 600 into service on November 30, 1965, and Caribair began operating the first Model 640 three weeks later on December 22. Hawaiian Airlines was in service with the Model 640 the next day. Additional aircraft continued to be delivered well into the 1970s.

Just as Convairliners continued in service into their fifth decade, the modifications also continued. Between 1991 and 1993, Kelowna Flightcraft of Kelowna, British Columbia, Canada, produced a "stretched," or lengthened turboprop 580. Known as the Convair 5800, it was made possible by the technical support and pre-design team led by Ladd Mastny at Convair in San Diego. Many of the 580, 600, and 640 conversions were still flying at the turn of the century.

CHAPTER SIX

THE LOCKHEED ELECTRA:

The Turboprop "Jet"

The story of the L-188 Electra spanned two eras, but the aircraft itself fit comfortably into neither. It was conceived in the piston-engine era, when its turboprop engines offered the promise of a hefty increase in performance. However, by the time it was born, the word "jet" was the buzzword that described the future of air travel. Indeed, operators nervously called the Electra a "jet" because of its turbine power. Eastern Airlines, National Airlines, Pacific Southwest Airlines, Australia's Ansett, and others actually painted the word "Jet" or "Prop-Jet" on their Electras.

The Electra was designed as a fast, medium-capacity, medium-range liner to accommodate the needs of the domestic network of American Airlines and Eastern Airlines. It was designed and tested in 1954–1955, but did not enter service until 1959—by which time turbojet airliners were already in operation. Although overshadowed by the turbojets and dogged by technical problems, the Electra *did* enjoy a modest career on the intended medium-capacity, medium-range routes through the 1960s and into the 1970s with many airlines.

Today, turboprop power has become standard for small, twin-engine airliners that carry fewer than 40 passengers on feeder routes of less than a few hundred miles. However, among the major first-tier airlines, the turboprop era was over quickly. At the beginning of the 1950s, the step from piston engines to turboprop engines for medium- to long-range airliners briefly seemed like an obvious one. However, the speed and power advantage offered by turboprops was quickly eclipsed by that which was offered to the airline industry by turbojet engines.

In Britain, where they first appeared, there were several important large, four-engine turboprop airliners, including the Vickers Viscount and the Bristol Britannia. Of these, the Viscount was the smallest and the first to fly. It carried under 50 passengers and it first flew in 1950. The Britannia, which first flew two years later, carried nearly 100 passengers and was seen as Britain's answer to the Lockheed Constellation and the Douglas DC-6. The Viscount was later succeeded by its 100-passenger cousin, the Vanguard, but not until the end of the decade, after the Electra was available.

The Viscount was actually the impetus for Lockheed deciding to become the first major American aircraft maker to develop a four-engine turboprop airliner. When Capital Airlines announced the purchase 60 Viscounts in 1954, there were no major American planemakers with turboprop airliners available. Capital had earlier approached Lockheed to create a four-engine short- to medium-range turboprop airliner, because the planemaker had been working with the Allison Division of General Motors to develop the T56 turboprop

An L-188 Electra in Lockheed corporate markings with the logos of airlines that had placed orders. During the flight test days of 1957–1959 there was still optimism that the Electra would find the same level of sales success as her sister, the Constellation.

engine for the planned YC-130 four-engine military transport. Lockheed did not choose to develop an aircraft for Capital's requirements but revisited the concept when American Airlines expressed an interest in such an aircraft.

By the time that the YC-130 made its first flight in August 1954, a month after the Boeing 367-80 jetliner prototype, the airlines in the United States were clamoring for "jets"—turboprops as well as turbojets. Over the course of the ensuing year, Lockheed worked out the details of its new turboprop airliner, which was provisionally designated as CL-310.

The wings of the new aircraft were similar to that of YC-130, but they were attached at the bottom, rather than the top, of the fuselage. The fuselage itself was a simple cylinder rather than being gracefully contoured like that of Lockheed's Constellation. It

was designed to accommodate up to 90 passengers, double that of the Viscount, but slightly fewer than a Super Constellation at maximum capacity. Its range would be greater than that of a Viscount and less than that of a Super Constellation—but it would be the fastest of the three.

By the summer of 1955, Lockheed was ready to launch its turboprop airliner, which was designated as Model L-188 and given the name "Electra," a tribute to the prewar twin-engine Lockheed Model 10 Electra. A propliner that first flew in 1934, the Electra helped establish Lockheed as an important maker of commercial aircraft. It was perhaps best known as the aircraft that Amelia Earhart used for her ill-fated around-the-world attempt in 1937.

The original Electra had a wingspan of 55 feet, and a wing area of 458.5 square feet. It was 38 feet 7 inches long and had a tail height of 10 feet 1 inch. It

weighed 10,300 pounds fully loaded and fueled, and had a service ceiling of 19,400 feet. It had a range of less than 1,000 miles with maximum payload, although Earhart's plane was retrofitted with additional fuel tanks to extend its range. In its typical configuration, the Model 10 carried just 10 passengers. It was powered by a pair of Pratt & Whitney Wasp radial piston engines.

Two decades later, the new, four-turboprop Electra had a wingspan of 99 feet, and a wing area of 1,300 square feet. It was 104 feet 6 inches long and had a tail height of 32 feet 10 inches. It weighed 113,000 pounds fully loaded and fueled, and had a service ceiling of 28,400 feet. It had a range of 2,200 miles with maximum payload.

Although it was the obvious choice, Lockheed looked at two British engine types before deciding on the commercial version of the Allison T56 engine that

it was already using in the C-130 program. These engines, designated as 501D-13 and equipped with Aeroproducts propellers, would each provide 3,750 eshp and better performance than the Napier Eland or the Rolls-Royce Dart.

The Electra would be delivered in two variants, the basic Model L-188A and a longer-range L-188C, which was developed concurrently with the L-188A. The primary differences were an increase in fuel capacity from 5,450 gallons to 6,490 gallons and a gross takeoff weight of 116,000 pounds. The missing L-188B designation was used by the manufacturer to distinguish the L-188Cs that were designed with a navigator station and an extra lavatory that were earmarked for overseas customers. These 22 aircraft were all delivered as L-188Cs.

By the middle of 1955, Capital was no longer an interested party, but in June and September,

A pair of L-188 Electras in Lockheed livery, circa 1959. Lockheed retained four Electras for company use, an unusually large number for a new type of airliner.

A "Prop-Jet" Electra in Lockheed livery, circa 1959. In retrospect, the need to use the word "jet" to sell the Electra seems to betray a sense of desperation.

respectively, American Airlines and Eastern Airlines each placed the orders that launched the Model L-188 Electra. American initially ordered 35, increased the order to 40, and cut it back to 35, while Eastern ordered and took delivery of 40. The two airlines were considered to be complementary rather than directly competitive, because American's routes were primarily east-west, and Eastern's were mainly north-south on the Eastern Seaboard.

Lockheed thought it would probably also be able to sell Electras to TransWorld Airlines (TWA) for several reasons. Lockheed chairman Robert Gross and Howard Hughes, who owned a 78 percent and controlling share in TWA, had a close personal relationship. Hughes and TWA had also been instrumental in developing Lockheed's most successful propliner, the Constellation, and had ordered significant numbers of most Constellation variants. In short, TWA was the best commercial customer that Lockheed had ever had. According to

A Lockheed L-188 Electra Prop-Jet in General Motors livery during engine tests in 1959. The engines were built by Allison, a General Motors subsidiary. This aircraft was the sixth Electra to be built. Out of the first six aircraft, only one went to an airline.

Jack Real, the Division Engineer in Lockheed's Engineering Flight Test Department, Gross phoned Hughes in September 1957 and told him "Howard, I've sold 40 Electras to Eddie Rickenbacker [of Eastern], and I've sold 35 to C. R. Smith [of American]. Maybe I could find *one* for you."

While Gross was merely joking and they both knew that TWA could have as many Electras as Hughes wanted, the mercurial Hughes became angry at the disrespect that Gross was showing, and the two men never spoke again.

To resolve the situation, Gross asked Real to intervene and help sell Electras to Hughes. Because both Real and Hughes were engineers, Gross sensed that they spoke the same language. After a strange first meeting on a dark Los Angeles street corner, Real spent many hours with Hughes, and allowed him to fly the Electra on numerous occasions. However, before TWA placed its order, Hughes lost his control of TWA when his shares were forced into a blind trust, and TWA management refocused its interest on the new jetliners.

The Electra would fly for the first time on December 6, 1957, three years after the Boeing 367-80 jetliner prototype, but two weeks before the first production-model Boeing 707-120. On its sides, the first Lockheed prototype aircraft would carry the words "Lockheed Prop-Jet Electra." The emphasis was on "Jet."

Of the first 14 aircraft built, 5 were designated as flight test aircraft, and the rest were earmarked for Eastern Airlines. The first four were for Lockheed's use and the sixth went to General Motors' Allison Division. Allison used the aircraft for several years for continued testing of the engines, and sold the aircraft to the Los Angeles Dodgers baseball team in 1961. Of the subsequent 20 aircraft, 7 went to American Airlines and the balance to Eastern. Two of Lockheed's four aircraft were sold to Cathay Pacific in 1959, and one was converted as the prototype of the P-3 Orion for the U.S. Navy.

After just over a year of flight testing, the Electra entered service three months *after* the 707-120, but half a year ahead of the Douglas DC-8. By the end of 1958, 23 Electras had been built and half had been

A Lockheed L-188 Electra in Northwest Airlines livery, circa 1959. The Northwest Electra fleet would suffer two major crashes in 1960 and 1961 in which there were no survivors.

delivered to Eastern or American. The first revenue-producing scheduled L-188A flight for Eastern Airlines occurred on January 12, 1959, between New York and Miami, and the first for American Airlines, between New York and Chicago, followed on January 23. American would have been first, had it not been for a pilot strike that crippled the carrier through the busy Christmas season. On its side, the first Eastern aircraft would carry the words "Fly Eastern's Prop-Jet Electra." Again, the emphasis was on "Jet."

With Electras rolling off the Burbank assembly line faster than one a week, four other customers would be able to introduce Electra service before the summer of 1959. Ansett of Australia received its first of two L-188As on February 27, National Airlines received its first of 14 on April 1, Braniff International

Airways took delivery of its first of nine on April 29, and Western Air Lines received its first of 12 on May 20. The first 56 Electras would all be of the L-188A type, and by the end of 1959, a total of 95 L-188As had been produced.

The L-188C Electra was launched on July 1, 1959, when Northwest Airlines took delivery of the first of its 18 L-188Cs. Both Northwest and Eastern received an L-188C on July 21, and 20 L-188Cs would be delivered by the end of the year. Capital Airlines, which had been operating its fleet Viscounts, ordered five L-188Cs, but cancelled, and these aircraft were sold to other customers. Capital itself was acquired by United Air Lines in 1961.

Following Eastern's lead, Ansett, National, and Braniff all used the words "Prop-Jet" on their fuselages, while both Eastern and Western used the word "Jet"—without the prefix—in the headlines of their advertising. Pacific Southwest Airlines, which received its first L-188C on November 6, simply marked the fuselage "Electra JET." Through the end of 1959, 32 L-188Cs were built.

A great deal of publicity naturally surrounded the introduction of the new "Prop-Jet." Both the manufacturer and the operators found it to be in their best interest to encourage a great deal of media attention. This, however, would quickly backfire.

On February 3, 1959, after less than a month in service, the highly publicized new turboprop airliner suffered the first of a dreadful series of highly publicized fatal crashes. At 9:30 p.m., American Airlines Flight 1015 was inbound to LaGuardia Airport in New York City in dense fog when the pilot misread the altimeter. Thinking he was at 500 feet, when he was actually at 50 feet, he crashed into the East River. Of the 72 people aboard, only 7 survived, including the copilot, the flight engineer, and two flight attendants.

A Lockheed L-188 Electra in the markings of Eastern Airlines, circa 1959. Eastern was the first airline customer on the Electra order books, and it was also the largest operator, with 40 ships.

Below

L-188 Electras on the Lockheed ramp in Burbank, California, circa 1959. By 1959 activity here had tapered off dramatically. Deliveries of all types would total just 437 aircraft that year, a decline from the postwar peak of 1,871 in 1953, and the lowest Lockheed production total since 1948.

Most drowned in the cold waters of the East River. Although pilot error was eventually found to be the cause of the crash, the fact that it came during the first month of service cast a dark shadow over the program that had both the manufacturer and the airlines doing heavy damage control.

The cloud from the New York crash had just barely started to lift when, on September 29, 1959, a Braniff L-188C, the fifth Electra delivered to the airline, lost its left wing when the number one engine wrenched off the wing. It crashed near Buffalo, Texas, at 11:10 p.m., killing all 6 crewmembers and all 28 passengers. The Civil Aeronautics Board, Lockheed, and Allison could not find the cause. The Civil Aeronautics Board was about to issue its report chalking

A Lockheed L-188 Electra in the popular smiling face livery used by Pacific Southwest Airlines (PSA) on various aircraft types during the 1960s and 1970s. The Electra was especially useful on PSA's South Lake Tahoe service because through the 1970s, jets were banned from this regional airport.

Left

A Lockheed L-188 Electra in Braniff Airlines markings, circa 1959. Braniff's fifth Electra, an L-188C, was lost over Texas in 1959 when the number one engine failed, destroying the wing. A second Braniff Electra was lost over Texas in 1968.

Far Left

A Lockheed L-188 Electra in the markings of the Federal Aviation Administration, circa 1959. The agency was the only U.S. government customer for the commercial version of the Electra, although the U.S. Navy would buy more than 500 examples of the P-3 Orion, a patrol plane based on the Electra airframe.

The second Lockheed L-188A Electra to be delivered to National Airlines. Receiving its first aircraft in 1959, National would retain the Electra in service until 1968.

the crash up to unknown causes when a third Electra crashed. At 2:38 p.m. on March 17, 1960, the first L-188C operated by Northwest Airlines departed Chicago for Miami. At about 3:15 p.m., between Tell City and Cannelton, Indiana, the right wing failed because of flutter induced by oscillation of the outboard engine nacelle. All 6 crewmembers and all 57 passengers died in the crash.

Three fatal crashes within roughly a year of service made the Electra an anathema to the flying public, and there were calls for grounding the aircraft entirely. The Civil Aeronautics Board called for airspeed restrictions, even though neither of the two aircraft that lost wings had been flying at excessive speeds.

Both Lockheed and Allison would conduct exhaustive tests to determine what had happened. Gradually, the evidence was pieced together. It was discovered that the engine-mounting structures within the nacelles were prone to fail as a result of a

A Lockheed L-188C in Northwest Airlines livery on final approach, circa 1960. The Minnesota-based carrier helped launch the L-188C variant, and ordered 18 such aircraft.

phenomenon known as "whirl mode oscillation." It was discovered that as they failed, the oscillation and flutter would increase, it would then become uncontrollable and tear the nacelle off the wing, resulting in the wing itself coming off the aircraft.

On May 12, 1960, Robert Gross met with representatives of all the airlines who had bought the Electra and told them that the problem had been cornered and that Lockheed would pay for the structural retrofit that would solve the problem. The benign-sounding Lockheed Electra Achievement Program, best known by its acronym "LEAP," would cost the company $25 million ($145 million in turn-of-the-century dollars) and would take until February 1961.

In the meantime, however, an American Airlines Electra on a routine approach to LaGuardia hit a dike and overturned on the runway edge on September 14, 1960. Two weeks later, on October 4, an Eastern Airlines Electra hit 80,000 starlings just as it was airborne on takeoff from Boston Logan Airport, and crashed, killing 62 of 72 people aboard. These accidents were not the fault of the aircraft, but two in rapid succession—after all that the Electra had been through—turned its reputation a shade darker.

A year later, on September 16, 1961, after the LEAP Program had concluded, a Northwest L-188C Electra crashed on takeoff from Chicago, killing all 37 people aboard. The aircraft had suffered a mechanical failure in the aileron primary control system due to an

A Lockheed L-188 Electra in the livery of Koninklijke Luchtvaart Maatschappij (KLM, Royal Dutch Airlines), circa 1965. The Netherlands flag carrier was Lockheed's only European customer for the Electra.

A Lockheed L-188 Electra in the markings of Garuda Indonesian Airways, circa 1959. Garuda maintained a working relationship with the airline of Indonesia's former colonial master, so Garuda often ordered the same aircraft types as Koninklijke Luchtvaart Maatschappij (KLM, Royal Dutch Airlines).

improper replacement of the aileron boost assembly. This resulted in a loss of lateral control at an altitude that was too low for the pilot to recover. A month before this crash, it had become routine maintenance to change the aileron boost package mounted on the aircraft rear beam. The boost package had cables that were secured with safety wire that went through a turnbuckle. Records showed that the Northwest inspector failed to inspect the safety wire installation. The airline, not the manufacturer, was found liable, but by then, it no longer mattered. For Lockheed, the program was over. The last Electra delivery had taken place on August 25, 1961, and there would be no additional orders.

Despite its growing negative reputation during the 1959–1961 period, and competition from turbojet aircraft, the Electra would serve successfully on most of its routes. Until the introduction of the Boeing Model 727 jetliner into airline service during 1964, the Electra was the fastest and newest aircraft available

for short- to medium-distance routes, and its operating career with most of its original users would continue into the 1970s.

Lockheed produced a total of 170 Electras, including 116 L-188As and 54 L-188Cs. Of the latter, 20 had been given the internal, unofficial designation "L-188B" before delivery as L-188Cs.

Eastern Airlines, the biggest Electra operator and the airline with the most accelerated delivery schedule, took delivery of 34 L-188As through July 9, 1959, and 5 additional L-188Cs between July 27 and October 14, 1959. These remained in front-line service only briefly, as Eastern began buying jetliners for its long-range operations in 1960. However, the Electras stayed in service for a long time, flying as part of Eastern's Air-Shuttle system from 1961 until 1977.

The other original Electra customer, American Airlines, would operate 35 Electras, all L-188As, with the last one delivered on March 21, 1960. American later briefly owned, but did not operate, the L-188A that had been produced as the test aircraft for Allison and later operated by the Los Angeles Dodgers. American was initially very successful with the Electra because its major competitors, United Air Lines and TWA, had neither jets nor turboprops. However, as jetliners began to come into the market in the mid-1960s, American began to dispose of its L-188As, which had disappeared from the fleet by 1971.

The third United States carrier to operate the Electra, National Airlines, received its last 2 of 14 L-188As from Lockheed on January 6 and 9, 1961, but it bought an additional 3 from American Airlines in 1962. Originally used on the route between New York and Miami that rivaled Eastern Airlines, National soon moved its Electras to other, shorter routes, even before the last aircraft were delivered from Lockheed. In 1961, when National extended its system to the West Coast, Electras were used to pioneer these routes. Despite the addition of Boeing 727 jetliners in 1964, National kept the Electras on its routes until 1968, when all were sold.

Braniff received its ninth and last L-188A January 9, 1960, but added one L-188C two years later. Completed on December 17, 1960, as part of the cancelled Capital Airlines order, it was delivered to Braniff on May 10, 1962. The Electra fleet remained with Braniff only through the end of the decade, when efforts were undertaken to make it an "all-Boeing" airline.

Western Air Lines received its 12th and last L-188A from Lockheed a month later on February 9 a month after the final Braniff delivery. Ultimately replaced by the new generation of small Boeing jetliners, Western's Electras would remain in service only until 1969.

PSA, whose operations were concentrated within California, had the type of route structure on the West Coast that was roughly analogous to that of Eastern's Air-Shuttle in terms of distances, population densities, and frequency of service. As such, the Electra proved to be an ideal aircraft, even when PSA made its transition to small jetliners. PSA eventually operated nine Electras, although only four were ordered directly from Lockheed. The first three of these were L-188Cs received in November and December 1959, while the fourth was an L-188C completed for Capital Airlines in April 1960 and sold to PSA in January 1962. The original fleet was phased out by 1969, but in 1976, PSA acquired its second round of Electras from American Airlines and other sources to service its route into South Lake Tahoe, where jets were not then permitted. These prop-jets would remain in operation until 1979.

The principal overseas customer for the Electra was the transport ministry of the Australian government, which mandated (for the sake of commonality) the acquisition of the aircraft by five airlines that it controlled down under. By the late 1950s, there was a perceived need to upgrade the fleets of medium-range aircraft flying the regional routes in the Southwest Pacific. The Electra would be chosen over the Vickers Viscount or the de Havilland Comet, even though a British aircraft was preferred for political reasons.

The airlines in question were Qantas (formerly Queensland And Northern Territories Air Service), the overseas national flag carrier of Australia; Trans-Australia Airlines (TAA); Tasman Empire Airways, Ltd. (TEAL); Australian National Airways (ANA); and Ansett. The latter two merged in 1957 to form Ansett-ANA, from which the "ANA" suffix was later dropped. TEAL, of which the government of New Zealand owned a share, would become Air New Zealand in 1965.

Ansett-ANA was the first to receive the Electra, taking delivery of three directly from Lockheed between February 1959 and February 1960. A fourth L-188A was later acquired from American Airlines. Originally operated on the short but high-density passenger route between Sydney and Melbourne, the Ansett Electras were returned to Lockheed in the early 1970s for factory conversion to freighters under the designation L-188AF. In this role, they operated on interisland flights throughout the Southwest Pacific. Retired in 1984, they were the last Electras in service with an original customer.

TAA took delivery of two L-188As in June and July 1959 and a third in August 1961. A fourth Electra operated by TAA, an L-188C, was actually on lease from Qantas. TAA operated its Electra fleet on passenger routes throughout the country until 1972, when operations were discontinued. Unlike the case with its rival domestic carrier Ansett, there were no cargo conversions.

Qantas was an early operator of the L-188C, accepting four between October 30 and December 12, 1959. These were used on longer over-water routes, including those to New Zealand, Singapore, Manila, and as far as Japan and South Africa with intermediate stops. Because these routes were better served by the faster, longer-legged Boeing 707 jetliners, Qantas disposed of most of its Electra fleet in the late 1960s, including the sale of two to TEAL/Air New Zealand. TEAL originally ordered three L-188Cs from Lockheed. With the addition of the two ex-Qantas aircraft

A Lockheed L-188 Electra in the livery of Ansett Airlines of New Zealand, circa 1959. Both Ansett and Australian National Airways (ANA) ordered the Electra, but they merged in 1957 and the "ANA" disappeared from the name by 1959. Ansett was the last of the original Electra operators still flying the type.

in 1965 and 1970, it operated a total of five, but never more than three at any given moment. The first TEAL Electra actually went into service in October 1959, before Qantas received its first one. The last Electras were retired by Air New Zealand in 1971 and 1972.

Lockheed's only European customer for the Electra would be the national flag carrier of the Netherlands, Koninklijke Luchtvaart Maatschappij (KLM, Royal Dutch Airlines). The airline received 12 L-188Cs between September 1959 and December 1960, using them on short- and medium-distance intra-European and Middle East flights, where they proved to be faster than Caravelle jetliners because of a shorter turnaround time. One KLM L-188C was lost in a fatal crash in Cairo on June 12, 1961, and the remaining aircraft were sold to the American air freight company, Universal Airlines, in 1968 and 1969.

In the Far East, Lockheed had two customers, Hong Kong-based Cathay Pacific and Garuda, Indonesia's national flag carrier. Garuda acquired three L-188Cs in January 1961 for service to destinations as far away as Tokyo. One was lost in a crash in 1967, and the other two were sold in 1972. Cathay Pacific bought two of Lockheed's flight test prototypes in April and June 1959 and operated them on routes throughout the Far East until the airline converted to jets in the late 1960s.

In addition to its airline customers, Lockheed took an order for one L-188C from Howard Hughes by way of his Hughes Tool Company. This order was subsequently canceled and Lockheed sold the Electra to the U.S. Federal Aviation Administration (FAA) in February 1961 for use in training and runway inspection. This aircraft was transferred to the National Air

& Space Administration (NASA) in 1978, and based at the space agency's Wallops Island, Virginia, space launch facility until it was scrapped in 1997.

There was no military transport version of the Electra, although Lockheed did adapt the Electra airframe for the highly successful naval patrol and antisubmarine warfare aircraft known to the U.S. Navy (and others) as the P-3 Orion and to the Canadian Armed Forces as the CP-140 Aurora. In February 1959, the U.S. Navy awarded Lockheed a contract to develop a replacement for the aging Lockheed P2V Neptune. Lockheed used the third L-188 airframe as the basis for the prototype, which first flew on August 19, 1958, under the designation YP3V-1. The first production Orion (Lockheed Model L-185) made its debut on April 12, 1961, under the designation P3V-1, which was changed to P-3A in 1962.

The first of 157 P-3As joined the fleet in 1962, and the improved P-3B was introduced in 1965. Production of the secondary type included 124 for the U.S. Navy, as well as 10 for the Royal Australian Air Force, and 5 each for the Royal New Zealand Air Force and the Norwegian Luftforsvaret (Air Force). While there have been numerous modified variants of the Orion, the final production version was the P-3C, which was first flown in the form of a modified P-3B, designated as YP-3C, in 1968. The U.S. Navy was the largest P-3C customer, but they were also sold to Australia, the Netherlands, Norway, Japan, Pakistan, and South Korea. Additional Orions were also built in Japan under license to Kawasaki. The Canadian CP-140 Aurora was a P-3C airframe that incorporated electronic gear from both the P-3C and the Lockheed S-3A Viking, including APS-116 search radar. In 1989, Canada began ordering a strippeddown version strictly for patrol duties under the designation CP-140A Arcturus.

The P-3C went through a staged series of three upgrade programs, culminating with the P-3C Upgrade III. The last of these rolled off the Lockheed production line in April 1990, although an Upgrade IV variant was produced later by Kawasaki in Japan using Japanese equipment. An Upgrade IV version of the Orion, designated P-7, was later considered and rejected by the U.S. Navy.

At the beginning of the twenty-first century, the Lockheed P-3C Orion was still the U.S. Navy's primary land-based, antisubmarine warfare patrol aircraft. It has advanced submarine detection sensors such as directional frequency and ranging (DIFAR) sonobuoys and magnetic anomaly detection (MAD) equipment.

The avionics system is integrated by a general-purpose digital computer that supports all of the tactical displays, monitors and automatically launches ordnance, and provides flight information to the pilots. In addition, the system coordinates navigation information and accepts sensor data inputs for tactical display and storage. The P-3C can carry a mixed payload of weapons internally and on wing pylons.

The P-3C Orion has a wingspan of 99 feet 7 inches, is 116 feet 8 inches long and has a tail height of 33 feet 8 inches. It has a gross takeoff weight of 139,760 pounds, and has a service ceiling of 30,000 feet. It is powered by four Allison T-56-A-14 turboprop engines, each delivering 4,600 eshp. It had a typical mission duration of 10 to 12 hours, with a maximum endurance of 14 hours and it carries a crew of 12. Armament consists of the AGM-84 Harpoon cruise missile, the AGM-65 Maverick air-to-ground missile, MK-46 torpedoes, depth charges, sonobuoys, and mines, up to a total payload of 20,000 pounds.

The electronic surveillance variant, designated as EP-3E ARIES (Airborne Reconnaissance Integrated Electronic System) became the center of an international incident when one such aircraft collided with a Chinese air force fighter in international airspace on April 1, 2001 and was forced to make an emergency landing on Hainan Island.

After being sold by the original customers, Lockheed Electras were used by many second- and thirdtier airlines around the world as passenger and cargo transports and as fire bombers. The largest secondary user of Electras in passenger configuration was Brazil's Varig (Viac Aerea do Rio Grande). Varig started acquiring secondhand Electras from American Airlines in September 1962, less than a year after the aircraft was in production at Lockheed. American had actually contracted in 1961 to dispose of several L-188As to Redes Estaduais Aereas Limitada (REAL), another Brazilian airline which was bought by Varig in 1961. Through 1970, Varig would acquire 15 Electras, making it the third largest operator of passenger Electras after American, Eastern, and Northwest. These would serve primarily between Brazil's two largest cities, Sao Paulo and Rio de Janeiro, whose combined population would grow to exceed 20 million during the three decades that they were served by Electras. Varig would retain the Electra in service until 1994.

The largest secondary operator of Electras and the second largest operator of any kind was the cargo carrier Zantop International Airlines, which was

A Lockheed L-188 Electra in the markings of KLM, Royal Dutch Airlines, circa 1959. For KLM, the Electra proved faster than the French-built Caravelle jetliner on round-trip flights because of its faster turnaround time.

known as Universal Airlines between 1966 and 1972. Through the years, Zantop/Universal operated a total of 38 Electras, most of them converted for cargo use by Lockheed. Through 1970, Universal acquired 13 Electras, including the 11 surviving KLM L-188Cs, but these were lost when the company went bankrupt in 1972. Re-emerging as Zantop, the carrier bought 25 used Electras from various sources, including Eastern Airlines, and two secondary users, Overseas National Airways and Hawaiian Airlines.

At the turn of the century, large numbers of military P-3s were still in service, but original commercial Electras were relatively few. In Canada, both Conair and Air Spray operated former Electras as aerial tankers and NASA still operated the former FAA Electra. The last regularly scheduled Electra passenger service was terminated by Reeve Aleutian Airways in 1999, but a number of Electra freighters were still seen around the world, especially the third world.

One such aircraft was the source of what may be the last great Electra anecdote. On December 18, 1995, a former Eastern Airlines L-188C registered to TransService Airlift but reportedly chartered by Angola's UNITA movement, crashed into a remote region of Angola, apparently en route to an undisclosed site in Zaire. It was overloaded with 144 persons, whose identity remained a mystery, and of whom only 5 survived. Zaire's transport minister, Alexis Thambwe Mwamba, said that the Electra crashed in the Cuango area, which was under UNITA control, and that it frequently landed at an airstrip close to the town of Luzamba. Rumors suggested that it was involved in diamond smuggling, because diamonds produced in Angola's remote Lunda Norte and Lunda Sul regions were reportedly being smuggled by way of Zaire, which is now known as the Democratic Republic of Congo.

CHAPTER SEVEN

THE RACE

to Launch the Jet Age

The advent of jetliners was the most important turning point in the history of air travel, yet this happened at a time when much of what we take for granted today was still an unproven theory.

Few milestones in aviation history were more momentous than the advent of turbojet propulsion, although, initially, its potential went unrecognized by anyone with the power to put it to use. Of course, such a thing is not unprecedented. The steam engine was invented by Denis Papin in 1685, but the first practical steam-powered vehicle, Robert Fulton's steamboat, was not operational until 1807. Fortunately, jet propulsion didn't take that long. Instead of lagging for more than a century, it merely lay dormant for about a decade.

The turbojet engine was invented by a British test pilot and Royal Air Force officer named Frank (later Sir Frank) Whittle. Archimedes discovered and recorded the principles of jet propulsion in the third century B.C., and Sir Isaac Newton wrote that "for every action, there is an equal and opposite reaction" in the seventeenth century. However, in 1928, the 21-year-old Whittle envisioned a practical engine, which he called a "turbojet," in which thrust could be generated by burning fuel in a combustion chamber. Air would be forced into the chamber ahead of the engine by a turbine so that the thrust of the hot gas ejected from the rear of the chamber would be greater than the flow of air into the front of the engine. Thus, forward motion would be generated.

Whittle patented his turbojet idea in 1930, but his bosses at the Royal Air Force and the leaders of the British aviation industry could see no practical use for Whittle's amusing little engine. Five years later, in Germany, Hans Pabst von Ohain patented a similar idea.

Over the next few years, though, Whittle managed to attract some investment capital from investors who could see the potential, and on March 2, 1936, he formed a company called Power Jets, with the expressed purpose of building a turbojet-powered aircraft. A month later, von Ohain, along with Max Hahn, began working toward exactly the same goal under the auspices of the Heinkel company in Marienehe, Germany. Whittle completed his first engine in 1937 but deemed it not "flight-ready," so von Ohain was the first to see his dream come true. His HeS3B engine became the world's first practical turbojet. On August 27, 1939, at Marienehe, the Heinkel He 178, powered by a von Ohain HeS3B, became the first jet-propelled aircraft to fly.

One of Pan American's long-range 707-321 jetliners. Having bought just 8 707-121s, Pan American acquired 26 707-321s, 60 707-321Bs, and 35 707-321Cs. Its total of 128 was the biggest in the program, although TWA was a very close second with 123 707s and 4 720s.

initial flight on May 15, 1941, in the Gloster E.28/29. The first American jet aircraft, the Bell XP-59 Airacomet, which debuted on October 3, 1942, was powered by a Whittle turbojet.

The dawn of jet propulsion coincided with World War II, so the first jet aircraft to go into operational service were combat aircraft. Germany's Messerschmitt Me 262, a two-engine fighter, made its maiden flight on July 18, 1942, and entered squadron service in June 1944. The first operational American jet fighter, the Lockheed P-80 Shooting Star, flew on January 8, 1944, and was followed four days later by the first operational British jet fighter, the Gloster Meteor. Neither the British nor the American aircraft actually entered air-to-air combat in World War II, but several German jets, including the Me 262, and the Arado Ar 234—with four turbojet engines—saw action before the war came to a close.

The potential of jet aircraft was recognized before the Me 262 became operational, but its success in combat demonstrated that major changes in aviation were coming. Even before the war ended, the air forces of the major powers had decided that their future combat aircraft would be jets, and the

An American Airlines Boeing 707 jetliner at Los Angeles International Airport, circa 1958. American was one of the first customers for the 707, placing its initial order on November 9, 1955, just three weeks after Pan American. It would be the first to operate transcontinental routes inside the United States and would ultimately buy 103 707s and 25 720s.

A Boeing 707-227, which was delivered to Braniff International Airways in October 1959. Braniff's history with the aircraft began with a December 1955 order and culminated in a total of 5 720s and 14 707s, the latter including 9 707-320C series aircraft.

In Italy, an entirely different type of jet engine was being developed in which an air compressor driven by a piston engine was used instead of a turbine. The Caproni Campini N-1 was successfully flown with this engine on August 28, 1940, but the system was deemed impractical because the airplane was slower than propeller-driven aircraft, and the idea was abandoned.

The first twin-jet aircraft, the Heinkel He 280, made its maiden flight on April 2, 1941. Frank Whittle's first successful turbojet engine finally made its

major aircraft manufacturers, especially in the United States and Britain, began to study the possibility of jet-propelled airliners that could speed passengers to their destinations in two-thirds or less time than piston engine airliners.

By the late thirties, before World War II began, the United States had emerged as the acknowledged world leader in commercial aircraft. As the war drew to a close, the American planemakers prepared to resume that position in the postwar world. Most of the competition was gone. France had been badly mauled. Germany, Italy, and Japan were defeated. The Soviet Union had little knack for anything commercial. This left only the British aircraft industry as a potential competitor.

Before the war ended, Lord Brabazon had chaired a committee to plan the postwar course of British aviation, looking at all the possibilities. Among these was a jet-propelled airliner, which, if successful, could make British industry a world leader.

While American industry, notably Douglas and Lockheed, returned to propliners and pushed ahead with commercially successful aircraft, British industry followed both paths. In July 1947, de Havilland formally announced the development of its DH-106 jetliner, named "Comet" after the famous de Havilland prewar racing planes. It was to be designed by Ronald Bishop, with engines designed by Frank Halford. Among its design challenges would be pressurization. While the American postwar propliners would be pressurized to

In this 1958 magazine ad, American Airlines touted the fact that it was the first carrier to operate the revolutionary new Boeing 707 *within* the United States. Pan American World Airways had been the first airline to operate the 707, but this service was between the United States and Europe. At the time, Pan American did not have routes within the United States.

A Douglas DC-8-62 in the colorful markings of Braniff International Airways. In the 1970s, the carrier commissioned noted modern artist Alexander Calder to create flamboyant color schemes for some of its aircraft.

A Douglas DC-8-21 in the markings of National Airlines, once known as the "Airline of the Stars." Many of the DC-8s originally sold to National were subsequently owned by Braniff.

permit them to fly above storm clouds, the Comet would have to be pressurized to fly above 30,000 feet, where its engines would be more efficient. Efficiency was important, because jetliners would have to match the range of propliners in order to be competitive.

The 36-passenger DH-106 Comet I made its first flight on July 27, 1949, ushering in the commercial jet age to the sound of four de Havilland Ghost 50 turbojets, each delivering 4,450 pounds of thrust. Over the next several years, the Comet demonstrator set numerous commercial speed records flying between London and various cities in Europe, Africa, and the Far East, where government-owned British Overseas Airways Corporation (BOAC) intended to put it into service. Other British Commonwealth airlines, such as Canadian Pacific Airlines, also placed orders for the world's first jetliner.

Regularly scheduled Comet service was inaugurated on May 3, 1952, with a BOAC flight from London to Johannesburg, South Africa, averaging 490 miles per hour. BOAC soon had Comets in service on other high profile routes, and it began to look as though the aircraft really *had* ushered in a new age in commercial aviation.

Suddenly, however, things started to go terribly wrong. Between October 1952 and the first anniversary of the debut flight, two BOAC Comets and one belonging to Canadian Pacific were lost. The third of

these incidents took place in Karachi on the first flight anniversary itself—and cost the lives of all 43 persons aboard. On January 10, 1954, the aircraft that had made the original debut flight suddenly burst into flames at 30,000 feet shortly after takeoff from Rome, and crashed into the Tyrrhenian Sea. The Comets were initially grounded, then allowed to resume service, but a series of inquiries concluded in February 1955 that structural fatigue problems were to blame. The high-profile Comet crashes served to convince much of the traveling public that jetliners simply weren't safe.

The manufacturer insisted that the newer and larger Comet Mk.III, which was introduced in 1954, had none of the structural deficiencies of the original model, but a shadow had fallen across the British commercial aircraft industry.

Turned off by the "Comet Curse," the world's airlines initially turned away from jetliners altogether, but finally, they turned to the Americans. By the time that the Comet Mk.IV (Comet 4), the production version of the Mk.III, entered service with BOAC in 1958, the larger, faster, and more reliable American jetliners were already setting the standard for the future of air travel.

At the same time that turbojet engines were being developed, so too were "turbopropeller," or "turboprop" engines. These engines work on the same principle as a turbojet engine, but transmit power to the air by means of a propeller rather than through the jet exhaust. In a turboprop engine, a conventional propeller is geared to the shaft of a gas generator composed of a compressor, burner, and turbine. The turboprop engine was lighter and simpler than the large high-power piston engines, such as the Pratt & Whitney Twin Wasp or the Wright Double Cyclone, which depended on multiple "layers" of cylinders and which were very complex to operate and maintain. Clearly, piston engine technology had reached the performance level beyond which it was no longer practical. Something else was needed. Would it be the turboprop, the turbojet, or both of these—and in what order?

A turboprop engine could develop twice the horsepower per pound of weight as a piston engine and it appeared to be more reliable and economical than a turbojet. In the early fifties, most airline and aircraft industry analysts predicted that there would be a substantial period of time when turboprop engines would be the principal means of propulsion for most leading edge commercial aircraft. Turbojets would eventually become standard, but only *eventually*, and it was believed that turboprops would reign supreme for at least a decade. In fact, turboprop airliners had not yet approached the point of replacing piston-engine propliners when practical turbojet airliners began reaching the market in substantial numbers.

Today, turboprop power has become standard for small, twin-engine airliners that carry fewer than 40 passengers on feeder routes of less than a few hundred miles. However, among the major first-tier airlines, the turboprop era began and ended quickly. At the beginning of the 1950s, the step from piston engines to turboprop engines for medium- to long-range airliners briefly seemed like an obvious one. However,

An in-flight view of the second Douglas DC-8-62 delivered to Swissair. The three "Super Sixty" series ships taken by the Swiss carrier included one convertible freighter.

the speed and power advantage offered by turboprops was quickly eclipsed by that which was offered to the airline industry by turbojet engines. While turboprops represented a great deal of improvement in speed and performance over conventional piston engines, they could never match the ultimate speed of a turbojet because of the limitations of a propeller as a means of propulsion. The propeller itself created aerodynamic drag.

As had been the case with jetliners, it was the British, rather than the American aircraft industry, that led the way into the world of turboprops. By the end of the 1940s, there were several major turboprop projects on British drawing boards. Probably the two most important large, four-engine, first-generation British turboprop airliners were the Vickers Viscount and the Bristol Britannia. Of these, the Viscount was the smallest and the first to fly. It carried under 50 passengers and made its debut in 1950. The Britannia, which first flew two years later, carried nearly 100 passengers and was seen as Britain's answer to the Lockheed Constellation and the Douglas DC-7. The Viscount was powered by four 2,100-eshp Rolls-Royce Dart engines, which gave it a cruising speed of 350 miles per hour, a substantial improvement over a typical propliner of the day.

The Bristol Britannia, powered by four 4,120-eshp Bristol Proteus engines, finally entered airline service in September 1957. With a top speed of just under 400 miles per hour, it was, for a brief moment, the state of the art, but a year later, the first Boeing jet-

A Douglas DC-8-32 in the livery of Northwest Airlines, with whom it first flew in 1960. Northwest was a marginal operator of DC-8s, choosing to equip itself mainly with Boeing planes.

This Convair 880, the 20th airframe of the series, was part of the Northeast Airlines order that was subsequently delivered to TWA and held in storage while Howard Hughes scrambled to get the financing to pay for it.

liner would be in service—and half again faster. The Viscount was later succeeded by its 100-passenger cousin, the Vanguard, but not until the end of the decade, after jetliners had changed commercial aviation forever.

At the time that de Havilland announced the Comet, most American aircraft manufacturers had considered the idea of jetliners, but none had a serious project under way. By the time that the Comet made its operational debut, however, both Boeing and Douglas had turned up the flame on their own in-house studies. The situation within the companies was quite different, however. Douglas was, and had been since the 1930s, the world's leading maker of airliners. Over half the world's airline passengers flew on Douglas equipment. Since World War II, Douglas had sold a dozen DC-4/DC-6 series aircraft for every four-engine airliner that Boeing sold. Among the makers of four-engine airliners in the United States, Boeing was a distant third behind Douglas and Lockheed.

Both Douglas and Lockheed had a momentum going with their propliner programs that was not matched at Boeing, where sales of the Stratocruiser were sluggish by comparison. In a sense, the Seattle planemaker had little to lose by beginning to work seriously on a jetliner.

When the Comets started falling out of the sky, Douglas saw this as a confirmation that they had made the correct decision in going forward with their DC-7 program, but Boeing pushed ahead. While Douglas and Lockheed feared the "Comet Curse," and decided to be safe rather than sorry, Boeing saw that the curse was on the *airplane* and not the *concept*.

Jetliners would not only change the world of aviation, but they would shrink the world itself. Because they could fly nearly twice as far and nearly twice as fast, jetliners shrank distances dramatically. This was a major conceptual change, because it opened new horizons to average people. The forbidding North Atlantic that had challenged Lindbergh and the others still challenged airline passengers in the early 1950s. You could take a propliner across the Atlantic, but you had to make refueling stops in forbidding places like Newfoundland or Iceland. These places were windy and cold most of the year and downright cruel in midwinter. The average person who really didn't *need* to fly the North Atlantic, didn't. With jetliners, it became possible to fly between the United States and Europe in half the flying time and a third of the trip time, when one considers the layovers. Average Americans could start to think *realistically* about a trip to Europe, something that had been done previously only by a select few.

The advent of jetliners in the late 1950s changed the face of air travel more than any other single technological innovation since the Wright brothers first started carrying passengers. Nor has there been a comparable technological leap since. In the 1960s, we imagined that supersonic air travel would be such

a leap, but it never caught on. With the exception of Concorde, which showed itself to be truly practical only on the North Atlantic route, jetliners were flying at the same speeds at the turn of the century as they were in the 1960s. The Concorde crash at Charles DeGaulle Airport near Paris on July 25, 2000, interrupted, and effectively ended, the era of supersonic travel that had been, at most, a mere footnote in the history of aviation.

Jetliners today have greater range than those of the 1960s, but most passenger miles today are flown on routes that could have been flown with the range of first-generation jetliners. Engines are quieter, more reliable, and more fuel efficient today, but none of the changes of the past half century has had the same revolutionary impact as did the introduction of jetliners in the first place.

The fact that there have not been comparable technological leaps since the 1960s would come as a surprise to the aviators of that time, who had seen aviation progress from biplanes to supersonic jets in less than a generation. Such leaps of technology were confidently predicted to continue. It was projected that most long-distance flights would be made in supersonic aircraft by 1980, and rocket-powered airliners would be carrying passengers into space and on to the moon by 2001. Technologically, this would have been possible, but culturally and economically, it was not. Society was not willing to put up with "sonic booms" over populated areas, so supersonic travel fizzled. Travel to the moon went from exciting to amusing to boring when it was discovered that there was nothing there. Even today, there are not enough passengers in the world who would buy enough tickets to make commercial lunar travel possible. And, of course, no one in the aviation industry predicted the enormous leap in fuel prices that took place in 1973–1974.

In retrospect, the advent of jetliners was not simply a point on the continuous evolution of air travel, it was *the* milestone in the evolution of air travel. Jetliners changed air travel in terms of time-to-destination, but they also changed the culture of air travel. Suddenly, quick, long-distance air travel was so practical that it became routine.

However, as it became routine, air travel had lost its glamour. In 1949 it had been possible for Boeing to market the Stratocruiser only as an all-first-class luxury liner. There were large, comfortable seats and legroom to spare. Pullman-style berths were available for passengers to put on their pajamas, lie down, and

An interesting period view of the passenger cabin of a Convair 880, circa 1959. The Pullman-like passenger accommodations of the propliner era had already started to fade from the minds of those who designed aircraft interiors.

sleep. Downstairs, there was a comfortable lounge where passengers could relax, have a drink, and feel as though they were in a railroad club car or even in someone's living room.

In 1959 the emphasis within the cabin was on passenger density. Jetliners changed not only the culture of air travel, but that of travel itself.

The two Convair 880 aircraft painted in Convair colors and used for initial flight tests were registered, and later delivered, to TWA. Although he couldn't pay for them, Howard Hughes demanded that Convair not sell them to anyone else.

CHAPTER EIGHT

THE BOEING 707:

The First of Its Kind

The Boeing Model 707 was the first American jetliner, the world's first economically successful jetliner, and it sold in bigger numbers than any airliner of any type that preceded it.

Although it set a course toward aviation's future, the forward-looking first "707" wore a "Model 367" designation, linking it to the Model 367 Stratofreighter of the past. The prototype Boeing jetliner was specifically the Model 367-80, known familiarly as the "Dash-Eighty." While it is a well-known aspect of aviation folklore that Boeing used the "367" designation to camouflage the jet transport project from its competitors, it actually did have its roots in the Model 367 program.

Boeing's jetliner project began as an exercise in adapting jet propulsion to the existing 367/377 family of piston-powered transports. It will be recalled that the Model 367 was the military version of the Model 377 Stratocruiser. Because of Boeing's desire to sell a military version of its new jet transport, the design studies had their roots in the 367 rather than 377 nomenclature.

The early C-97 and KC-97 Stratofreighters, up through the KC-97E, had model numbers from 367-1 through 367-5, with KC-97F and KC-97G being Model 367-76. The intervening model numbers included numerous designs that never got off the drawing board, including many turboprop conversions between Model 367-22 and 367-60. Model 367-60 featured swept wings, with a 16 degree sweep, but its tail and fuselage were stock Model 367. Models 367-63 and 367-73 increased the wing sweep to 18 degrees and added a tail that was a clear forerunner to that of the Model 707.

By 1951, Boeing's Model 367-64 combined swept wing and tail surfaces with turbojet propulsion. The four engines were paired in nacelles borrowed from the swept-wing B-47 Stratojet bomber (Boeing Model 450) that Boeing was developing at that time for the U.S. Air Force. The fuselage was still almost exactly that of the familiar Stratocruiser, but the rest of the airframe looked ahead toward the future jetliner. The blunt nose of the 367/377 family was then changed to the bullet-like configuration of the B-47, but instead of the tandem fighter-plane-like seating of the B-47, Boeing designers retained the familiar side-by-side seating for pilot and copilot. The four engines were moved

A Boeing 707-123, one of the 707-100 series aircraft delivered to American Airlines in August 1959. Although the aircraft was scrapped in 1984, its nose section is still on formal public display in Germany.

The first Boeing 707-121 delivered to Pan American World Airways, the launch customer for the jetliner family. Its initial order on October 13, 1955, culminated in a total buy of 128 aircraft.

apart into separate nacelles and the resulting design was designated 367-80. This version was approved, and Boeing president Bill Allen gave his engineering department the green light to cut metal for a prototype, whose development was formally announced on August 30, 1952.

The company would invest $16 million in the project, betting on the future course of commercial aviation. Of course, there was a strong interest from the U.S. Air Force, which was extremely anxious for a jet transport that could be used as an aerial refueling aircraft. The new generation of fast jet bombers would soon be replacing the piston engine bombers in the Strategic Air Command, and the KC-97s would have a hard time keeping up with them.

The 367-80 had a wingspan of 130 feet, with the wings swept at 35 degrees, and a wing area of 2,402 square feet. It was 128 feet long and had a tail height of 38 feet 4 inches. It weighed 160,000 pounds fully loaded and fueled, and had a service ceiling of 42,000 feet. It was powered by four Pratt & Whitney JT3P turbojets, each delivering 11,000 pounds of thrust. It was only 18 feet longer than the Stratocruiser, but its gross weight was nearly 25 percent greater, and it could fly twice as fast.

The Model 367-80 Dash-Eighty rolled out the factory door at Boeing's Renton, Washington, facility on May 14, 1954, less than two years after the initial

announcement. Its first flight on July 15 marked the 38th anniversary of the Boeing Company. The new aircraft, which was dramatically different in appearance from any civilian aircraft before it, attracted a great deal of media attention, filling headlines and editorial pages throughout the world during an era when people were excited by the promise of technology. The Dash-Eighty also set new nonmilitary speed records each time it flew. This was illustrated March 11, 1957, when it streaked nonstop from Seattle to Baltimore—on a press demonstration flight—in three hours and 48 minutes, at an average speed of 612 miles per hour.

The Dash-Eighty served as the prototype for both civilian and military jet transports, whichwere designated as Model 707 and 717, respectively. The idea of giving Boeing jet transports model numbers beginning and ending with "7" was born by accident. By this time, Boeing had used up the 300 and 400 series of model numbers and had reserved the 500 and 600 series for nonaircraft projects, such as missiles. The new 700 series had just begun, so 707 was close to actually being the next available number. It sounded good, so Boeing reached ahead to 717, giving the two aircraft a relationship that was analogous to the 367/377 relationship of the previous aircraft. The rest, as they say, is history.

The initial civil variant was the 707-120, and the first military version was the 717-100. The first orders came from the U.S. Air Force, which ordered 29 717-100s in fiscal year 1955 and 68 717-146s the following year. The aircraft received the military designation KC-135A, and, as expected, they were all earmarked as aerial refueling aircraft. Their official given name was Stratotanker. Over the next seven years, the Air Force acquired an additional 627 717-148s as KC-135A Stratotankers and 18 717-157s as C-135A Stratolifters, a straight transport version that could be converted to tankers in the future.

The KC-135A/C-135A had a wingspan of 130 feet 10 inches, and a wing area of 2,433 square feet. It was 136 feet 3 inches long—8 feet longer than the Dash-Eighty—and had a tail height of 38 feet 4 inches. It weighed 297,000 pounds fully loaded and fueled, and had a service ceiling of 41,000 feet. It was powered by four Pratt & Whitney J57 turbojets, each delivering 13,750 pounds of thrust, giving it a cruising speed of 600 miles per hour. It had a ferry range of 5,000 miles and the KC-135A had an off-loadable capacity of 31,200 gallons of fuel.

Between 1961 and 1963, the U.S. Air Force ordered 30 717-158s under the designation C-135B and 17 Model 717-166s under the designation KC-135B. These "B"-type 717 aircraft differed from their "A"-type predecessors in that they were powered by Pratt & Whitney TF33-P-5 turbojets delivering 18,000 pounds of thrust. There were also 12 Model 717 tankers built for France under the designation C-135F (not KC-135F). The RC-135A and RC-135B electronic reconnaissance versions, with their large, nose-mounted radomes, were actually so different internally and electronically that they were developed by Boeing as Model 739 rather than as 717 variants. There were

10 739-445s and four 739-700s built, and these received various suffixes to their RC-135 designation as they were modified throughout their service careers. The U.S. Air Force 717 fleet also received numerous modifications and redesignation throughout more than a half-century of service, but the details of these specialized military variations are beyond the scope of the present work.

The first civilian orders for the 707-120 came from Pan American World Airways and American Airlines on October 13 and November 9, 1955, respectively. Juan Trippe, Pan American's president, announced that his airline would be spending $296

Five 707-120 series jetliners clustered around United Air Lines' Concourse B Spoke at San Francisco International Airport, circa 1961. This elaborate facility, featured briefly in the 1968 Steve McQueen film, *Bullitt*, was demolished long ago as part of the airport's continuous remodeling effort.

Clipper Fair Wind, a Boeing 707-321 delivered to Pan American World Airways in 1959. As with many of its given names, the carrier would reassign the *Clipper Fair Wind* to additional aircraft, in this case a Boeing 727 and a pair of Boeing 747s.

A color in-flight view of the first Boeing 707 to be equipped with the General Electric/SNECMA (Société National d'Etudes et Construction de Moteurs d'Avion) CFM56 series high-bypass turbofan engine.

million on Boeing 707s, in what was, at the time, the largest single order ever placed for commercial aircraft. Braniff Airlines placed its first order on December 1, 1955, followed by Continental Airlines on December 12.

Making its first flight on December 21, 1957, the Model 707-120 had a wingspan and wing area identical to the KC-135A/C-135A, but it was almost 10 feet longer at 145 feet 1 inch. The tail height was 41 feet 8 inches, and it had a gross weight of 248,000 pounds. The service ceiling was 41,000 feet, and the range was 3,000 miles, easily enough for the North Atlantic and transcontinental routes. It was powered by the civilian equivalent of the J57, four Pratt & Whitney JT3C-6 turbojets, each delivering 13,500 pounds of thrust, giving it a cruising speed of 600 miles per hour.

The 707-120 had a maximum passenger capacity of 181 persons, which was about three times that of a typically configured Stratocruiser. The 707-120 had the largest passenger cabin of any airliner yet flown, and the company was proud of the fact that the placement of its more than 100 windows allowed airlines to rearrange seats to change configuration. The location of passenger doors on the left side, and at the front and at the rear of the cabin, became standard for subsequent Boeing jets. The initial list price for the 707-120 was $5.5 million, although quantity discounts were available.

Meanwhile, in June 1955, Douglas had announced the decision to proceed with development of its own

In 1959, TWA advertised the fact that it offered service between New York and London on the Boeing 707, although it was not among the first to do so. Indeed, the aerial turnpike between these two cities would quickly become the signature route for the 707.

Boeing assigned the 707-220 designation to a short-range version of the 707-120 jetliner. For marketing reasons, the aircraft would make its debut as the Boeing Model 720. It served as a short-lived interim substitute for the Boeing 727 series.

jetliner, the DC-8, and it was widely believed in the industry that the first jetliner in service would take the bulk of future orders. Boeing knew it would have to hurry to get 707s into service before the competition arrived. This effort was successful.

Pan American was the first to put the new Boeing 707-120 jetliner into scheduled service, with a debut flight from New York to Europe on October 26, 1958. Within six weeks, Pan American's 707-120s had carried 12,168 passengers across the North Atlantic, and the airline had leased one of its jetliners to National Airlines for use on its New York to Miami route.

On January 25, 1959, American Airlines was the first of several U.S. airlines to start offering 707 jetliner service between New York and the West Coast. In its first year, the Boeing 707-120 carried a million

passengers for nearly a dozen airlines in Europe and the United States. The first scheduled service for the Douglas DC-8 would not occur until June 1959. Boeing had won the jetliner race.

Of the major U.S. airlines of the era, both Pan American and American Airlines had made early commitments to Boeing, while United and Eastern Airlines pledged to the DC-8. TransWorld Airlines (TWA), which had invested heavily in the Lockheed L-1649 Starliner, the ultimate Constellation, postponed a major acquisition of jetliners longer than the others but eventually went with Boeing.

Meanwhile, in 1957, Boeing had announced the second variant of its jetliner. Officially designated as Model 707-220, it was marketed as the Model 720, to give it the appearance of being a distinctly new

aircraft, which it really was not. Placed into service in 1960, the Model 720-100 was essentially a smaller, shorter-range version of the Model 707-120 that was designed to take advantage of jet speed on shorter routes, such as between San Francisco and Los Angeles, New York and Chicago, or Chicago and the West Coast. The 720-100 was essentially the same size as the 707-120 except for being 9 feet 8 inches shorter, with a maximum capacity of 167 passengers. It was powered by four Pratt & Whitney JT3C-7 turbojets, each delivering 12,500 pounds of thrust.

United Air Lines, which had been the first customer to put the Douglas DC-8 into service, was also the first to buy the Boeing 720, with the first of 29 ordered on November 22, 1957. Other orders came

from American Airlines on July 30, 1958, and Aer Lingus on March 11, 1959. The second foreign order came from Lufthansa on February 1, 1960. The second largest order, after that from United, was for 27 720s by Western Air Lines on February 12, 1960. Eastern Airlines, meanwhile, ordered 15. The first United Air Lines 720 began flying on the route between Los Angeles and Denver on July 5, 1960. Although a total of 154 720s were built, the service life of the type would be relatively short with major airlines, for within a few years, it would be replaced on shorter routes by Boeing's extremely successful Model 727 trijet.

Shortly after it began taking orders for the 707-120, Boeing announced the Model 707-320, which was seen as the ultimate member of Boeing's first generation family of jetliners. Whereas the 720 was be the

A Boeing 720 in the markings of Eastern Airlines, circa 1964. Primarily a regional carrier in the early 1960s, Eastern bought 15 Model 720 aircraft but no 707s. The airline later bought 163 727 aircraft from Boeing.

LUFTHANSA

shorter-range member of the family, the 707-320 would have longer legs than even the 707-120. The 707-320 was marketed as the "Intercontinental," because its 4,200-mile range was not only more than adequate for nonstop service on the high-density North Atlantic route, but it was sufficient to bring Asia within non-stop range of Europe.

The 707-320 was larger in all dimensions than its predecessors. It had a wingspan of 142 feet 5 inches, a wing area of 2,892 square feet, and a tail height of 41 feet 8 inches. At 152 feet 11 inches, it was nearly 7 feet longer than the 707-120 and 24 feet longer than the Dash-Eighty. This gave it a passenger capacity of up to 189. The Model 707-320 had a gross weight of 316,000 pounds, nearly double that of the Dash-Eighty. It was powered by four Pratt & Whitney JT4A turbojet engines, each delivering 15,800 pounds of thrust, giving it a cruising speed of 600 miles per hour, like its predecessors.

In the United States, both American Airlines and Pan American, who had helped launch the 707-120, placed orders for the 707-320, and Pan American would ultimately own 120 of the Intercontinentals and just 8 707-120s. Many foreign carriers, anxious to compete globally in a new age of air transportation, bypassed the 707-120 entirely and ordered the 707-320 even before the 707-120 went into service. The assumption was that they would be worth the wait. The first overseas sales were to Belgium's flag carrier, Sabena, and Air France, who both placed their orders on December 28, 1955. Both of these carriers were looking not only at the busy North Atlantic, but at establishing fast, efficient links to their colonies in Africa.

Five years later, during the summer of 1960, as Belgium's colonial mastery over the former Belgian Congo came to a bloody end, the Sabena 707s were the centerpiece of an effort that evacuated 15,000 people to Europe in two weeks. On some flights, the 707s carried as many as 300 passengers.

Major foreign orders for the Model 707-320 series that were received during 1956 came from Lufthansa on April 24, Air India on August 31, and British Overseas Airways Corporation (BOAC) on October 24. The last-mentioned acquisition was particularly important because Britain's national flag carrier had chosen an American jetliner over the British-made Comet 4, which de Havilland was struggling to have ready in order to compete with the Boeing aircraft. When BOAC opted for 15, instead of an expected 6 Boeings, it was seen as an endorsement of the American product over that of the British planemaker. Even though BOAC also bought the Comet 4, it was a turning point for the British aviation industry. While the Comet 4 did finally enter service with BOAC the same month as the 707-120, it carried fewer than half the passengers.

In 1961, after just 69 orders for the basic Model 707-320, Boeing introduced the Model 707-320B, which was powered by the Pratt & Whitney JT3D series turbofan engine. Pratt & Whitney's first commercial ducted bypass jet engine, it delivered 18,000 pounds of thrust. The wingspan was increased to 145 feet 9 inches, with a wing area of 3,010 square feet. The gross weight was raised to 336,000 pounds, which allowed more fuel, and which, in turn, increased the range to 6,160 miles.

In addition to the Model 707-320B, Boeing introduced the JT3D-powered Model 707-320C, which was the same size as the 707-320B, but was convertible between an all-passenger and all-cargo configuration, or any combination of the two. Pan American launched the convertible series in April 1962 with an initial order for 15 (under the designation 707-321C) that would later be increased to 34.

The sales totals for the latter two 707-320 subvariants would be 170 for the 707-320B and 306 for the 707-320C, making them the most popular of all Model 707 types.

As an inducement to BOAC to buy its Model 707 jetliner series, Boeing had created a new version, designated as the Model 707-420 series, which was identical to the 707-320B, except for its being powered by four British-made Rolls-Royce Conway Mk.508 turbofan engines delivering 17,500 pounds of thrust. BOAC took delivery of 10 707-320 series aircraft and 20 in the 707-420 series. The first of the latter would be delivered on May 19, 1959, under the designation 707-436. Other purchasers of the 707-420 type included Air India, which bought six;

Lufthansa, which bought five; and Israel's El Al, which bought three.

Another Rolls-Royce–powered variant to enter service in 1959 was the Model 707-138, which was a Model 707-120 airframe with the British-made engines. It entered service with Qantas in July between Sydney and London, with stops in Fiji, Honolulu, San Francisco, and New York. BOAC would inaugurate Boeing 707 service between London and New York in May 1960.

On March 7, 1965, a Qantas 707-320B (actually a 707-338B subtype) established a new distance record of 7,424 miles, becoming the first commercial aircraft in history to cross the Pacific Ocean nonstop. The flight, from Sydney to San Francisco, took 14 hours and 33 minutes.

Although all the 707 subvariants had suffixes ending in zero, each customer had its own suffix to the suffix, which was derived from a number added to the basic subtype number. For example, Pan American's number was "1," so its aircraft became 707-121, 707-321, and so on. The assigned numbers ranged up to "16" for BOAC, giving it aircraft such as the 707-436; and "18" for Qantas, giving it the 707-338, etc.

Production of the Model 707 family for commercial customers continued through 1978. All together 725 were built, including all Model 707/720 variants. The three largest operators were American Airlines and Pan American, with 128 aircraft each, followed by TWA with 127 and Northwest Airlines, with 49. The largest non-U.S. operators were Air France, with 38 aircraft and Sabena with 37.

The remainder of the Model 707/720 aircraft sold by Boeing to airline customers included 7 to Aer Lingus, 6 to Aerolineas Argentinas, 11 to Air India, 7 to Air Portugal, 3 to Airlift International, 2 to Alia, 5 to Avianca, 19 to Braniff, 2 to British Caledonian, 30 to BOAC, 1 to British Eagle, 10 to the Civil Air Authority of China (CAAC), 1 to Cameroon Airlines, 2 to China Airlines, 27 to Continental, 13 to Eastern Airlines, 5 to

A Boeing 720B in the livery of Northwest Airlines on final approach, circa 1965. Unlike many other carriers, Northwest ordered 13 720s before it ordered any 707s. In 1962 the 720s were augmented by 36 707s.

Ethiopian Airlines, 4 to Flying Tiger, 4 to Iranair, 3 to Iraqi Airways, 1 to Korean Air Lines, 5 to Kuwait Airways, 1 to LAN-Chile, 1 to Libyan Arab Air Lines, 31 to Lufthansa, 4 to Middle East Airlines, 3 to Malay/Singapore Airlines, 3 to Nigeria Airways, 6 to Olympic Airways, 2 to Pacific Northern, 11 to Pakistan International, 1 to Pertamina of Indonesia, 34 to Qantas, 8 to Saudia, 2 to Seaboard World, 10 to South African Airways, 2 to Sudan Airlines, 2 to Transporturile Aeriene Romaine (TAROM) of Romania, 29 to United Air Lines, 9 to Varig, 32 to Western Air Lines and 9 to World Airways.

Most of these aircraft were ordered in the early- to mid-1960s, but TAROM, Sudan Airways, and Iraqi Airways all placed their first orders in 1973. The last airlines to acquire the Model 707 were Pertamina and Libyan Arab, who placed their orders in December 1974 and July 1976, respectively. By this time, there were so many 707 airframes on the used aircraft market that Boeing terminated production of new airliners.

There were however, numerous nonairline customers, mostly governments, for the Model 707 airframe. Through the years, these added up to 131 additional aircraft. The U.S. government bought 46 Model 707/720 airframes, including one 720 for the Federal Aviation Administration and six for the U.S. Navy. The largest nonairline customer was the U.S. Air Force, which bought 39 Model 707 airframes directly from Boeing, in addition to the 820 Model 717 airframes that were delivered under the C-135 designation with various prefixes and suffixes.

Distinct from the Model 717/C-135 aircraft in the U.S. Air Force, the Model 707 aircraft were originally designated as C-137, with various prefixes and suffixes, although the majority were delivered as E-3s.

The most famous of the Air Force 707s were five VIP transports ordered with the "V" prefix. On May 14, 1958, three 707-153 (707-120 series) airframes were ordered under the designation VC-137A. The three VC-137As were subsequently re-engined with Pratt & Whitney TF33-P (JT3D-3) turbofan engines and redesignated as VC-137B. Completed with 22-passenger executive interiors, the VC-137s were intended as airborne command posts, but were permanently assigned to the 89th Military Airlift Wing at Andrews AFB near Washington, D.C., for the use of the president of the United States and high-ranking government officials.

The presidential VC-137A made its debut under the call sign *Air Force One* on August 26, 1959, when it carried President Dwight Eisenhower to Europe for conferences in Bonn, Paris, and London. It had the distinction of being the first jet assigned for the use of the president of the United States. Eisenhower nicknamed the aircraft *Columbine III*, after *Columbine II,* the Lockheed VC-121 Super Constellation that he had previously used as his presidential executive aircraft.

Eisenhower continued to use his VC-121 for some flights, and when John F. Kennedy became president in 1961, he used a Douglas VC-118 for many official flights because some runways in the United States were then still too short for jetliners.

The first aircraft specifically ordered for use as an executive transport for the president of the United States was a Model 707-353 (707-320B) ordered in 1962 under the designation VC-137C. This aircraft, tail number 62-6000, was delivered in the blue and white color scheme that is credited to Jacqueline Kennedy, and which is still standard for all presidential aircraft. It was 62-6000 that carried President Lyndon Johnson and the body of President Kennedy back to Washington after Kennedy's assassination in Dallas on November 22, 1963.

A second, more updated VC-137C, tail number 72-7000, was delivered to the 89th Military Airlift Wing in 1972. This aircraft was the official *Air Force One* of Presidents Richard Nixon, Gerald Ford, Jimmy Carter, Ronald Reagan, and George Bush. In 1990, during Bush's term, it was retired and replaced by a Boeing 747-200 airframe under the designation VC-25A.

The largest single order for noncommercial Model 707 airframes was for the aircraft designated by the U.S. Air Force as E-3A, but best known by its acronym AWACS, meaning Airborne Warning And Control System. Two of these aircraft were Model 707-320 airframes originally in 1971 under the designation EC-137D, but the order was expanded to 34 aircraft and the designation was changed before any were delivered. In addition to those for the U.S. Air Force, 18 707 AWACS were delivered to the North Atlantic Treaty Organization (NATO), 13 to Saudi Arabia, 7 to the United Kingdom, and 4 to France.

Known by its official (and aptly descriptive) name, "Sentry," the E-3A was the most sophisticated airborne command post ever devised. The idea dates back to the Vietnam War, when the U.S. Air Force operated Lockheed EC-121Q *College Eye* and EC-121R *Igloo White* Batcats over Laos and the Gulf of Tonkin and had great success in controlling and directing air operations against North Vietnam. After

Kay-O II, the Boeing 720B operated by the Los Angeles Dodgers baseball team. When still in Brooklyn, the team had used a Convairliner. The move to California brought them into the jet age.

the war, a revolution in the world of electronics made possible far more sophistication in much less space, so the Air Force went to even *more* space and the capability that it provided. The Model 707 airframe was designed to be configured with leading edge, state-of-the-art electronics and then topped with a 30-foot rotating radome, or "rotodome." The first of two dozen E-3A Sentrys were delivered in 1977, and they entered service on the first day of 1979. Although owned and flown by the Air Force Tactical Air Command, their first, and continuing, assignment was with the joint American-Canadian North American Aerospace Defense Command (NORAD).

The first E-3 Sentry entered U.S. Air Force service in March 1977 and the last was delivered in June 1984. NATO deliveries began in early 1982, and the 18th and last NATO E-3 was delivered in 1985. The NATO aircraft are staffed by crewmembers from various NATO member countries, but are all officially registered to the air force of Luxembourg. The Saudi E-3s were ordered in 1981 under the Peace Sentinel program, which ultimately included five E-3 AWACS aircraft and eight E-3 derivative aircraft designated KE-3 that had the capability of serving as aerial refueling tankers. These were the only Sentrys that were built with this capability. All of the Saudi aircraft were delivered between June 1986 and September 1987.

In 1986 the United Kingdom Ministry of Defence evaluated the E-3 as a replacement for its Nimrod airborne early warning system. The Boeing aircraft was chosen over an improved version of the Nimrod aircraft, which is, ironically, based on the old de Havilland Comet airframe. In February 1987, the governments of both the United Kingdom and France announced their planned acquisition of E-3 AWACS aircraft. The first aircraft were delivered to both countries during the spring of 1991, France received its final E-3 in February 1992, and the United Kingdom deliveries were complete in May 1992.

The U.S. Air Force, NATO, and Saudi E-3s are powered by four Pratt & Whitney TF-33-PW-100A turbofan engines delivering 21,000 pounds of thrust. The powerplant for the British and French aircraft is the General Electric/SNECMA CFM-56-2 turbofan, with 24,000 pounds of thrust.

The E-3 is the same length as the stock 707-320, with a slightly greater wingspan of 145 feet 9 inches, and a gross weight of 335,000 pounds. The AWACS aircraft carry a flight crew of four, plus 13 to 17 AWACS specialists depending on configuration.

Continually upgraded during the 1980s and 1990s, the Sentry's electronic systems include the Joint Tactical Information Distribution System (JTIDS) with its TADIL-J Tactical Digital Information Link and the ability to use the Global Positioning Satellite

system to pinpoint AWACS' location anywhere in the world. Electronic Support Measures (ESM) include a passive listening and detection system, which enables the AWACS to detect, identify, and track electronic transmissions from ground, airborne, and maritime sources. Using the ESM system, mission operators can determine radar and weapon system type.

The E-3 Sentry had its baptism of fire in 1991 during the Gulf War, when the airborne control services it offers proved vital in the management of the massive Coalition air armada. There were 11 U.S. Air Force and 5 Saudi AWACS aircraft operating over Saudi Arabia, supplemented by 3 more American E-3s from air bases in Turkey. Initially, their role had been a defensive monitoring of enemy air activity, but when the Coalition air strikes began against Iraq, the role shifted to a variety of tasks including surveillance, directing air strikes, interdiction of Iraqi airplanes, coordination of air-to-air refueling flights, and protection of high-value aircraft conducting intelligence and ground surveillance.

Between 1992 and 1995, British, French, and NATO E-3s were a major factor in the United Nations' ability to monitor and enforce the "no-fly" zone over Bosnia-Herzegovina. During the 1999 war in Kosovo, a multinational AWACS force helped direct NATO air actions against Serbian (Yugoslav) forces.

Another Model 707-320 airframe to gain notoriety during the Gulf War was the E-8 Joint Surveillance Target Attack Radar System (Joint STARS). It was developed for the U.S. Air Force and Army by Northrop Grumman using "pre-owned" 707-320 airframes rather than ones delivered from the Boeing factory. While the E-3 can monitor air activity over the battlefield, the E-8 has the capability of electronically monitoring battlefield activity on the ground. The E-8 is equipped with a sophisticated multimode radar, immense computer processing power and memory, and an elaborate communications suite. From an orbit far back in friendly airspace, the E-8C can detect, locate, classify, and track both fixed and moving surface targets in all weather conditions. On January 11, 1991, the only two Joint STARS aircraft then in existence were deployed to Saudi Arabia at the request of General Norman Schwarzkopf, commander of all Coalition forces in the Gulf, to support operations during Desert Storm. Under a 1985 contract, the Joint STARS aircraft were technically still being tested and were not ready for deployment in 1991 when they were pressed into service.

The final Model 707 in production was the U.S. Navy's E-6 Mercury, best known by its acronym, TACAMO ("Take Charge And Move Out"). Originally, the E-6A was an airborne communications system designed to link the National Command Authority (meaning the president and the top military leadership) with the U.S. Navy's submarine ballistic missile forces during times of crisis. Since 1998, the E-6As have been incrementally upgraded to E-6B standard, expanding their duties as a replacement for the U.S. Air Force's Airborne Command Post aircraft, due to the age of the EC-135 fleet. The E-6B is a dual-mission aircraft capable of fulfilling either the E-6A mission or the airborne strategic command post mission and is equipped with an airborne launch control system (ALCS). The ALCS is capable of launching United States land-based intercontinental ballistic missiles.

The Mercury carries a very low frequency communication system with dual trailing wire antennas. Excluding the antenna, the aircraft is 150 feet 4 inches long, with a wingspan of 148 feet 4 inches, and a tail height of 42 feet 5 inches. It has a gross weight of 342,000 pounds, and is powered by four General Electric/SNECMA CFM-56-2A-2 high-bypass turbofan engines.

The Navy accepted the first E-6A in August 1989, and the first E-6B upgrade became operational in October 1998. The last E-6 was the last 707 ever manufactured. A Model 707-320 airframe, it was delivered on September 9, 1992. It had been 14 years since the delivery of the last commercial 707 airframe and 38 years since the first flight of the original series prototype.

Although the final delivery was in 1992, Boeing officially closed the Model 707 production line in May 1991, and it was dismantled as the last E-6 moved through it.

In those 38 years, Boeing built 855 Model 707 airframes, 154 Model 720 airframes, 820 Model 717 airframes, 14 Model 739 airframes, and the 1 Model 367-80 prototype.

In January 1998, Boeing reassigned the 717 model number to the commercial line for the 717-200 regional jetliner, which had formerly been designated MD-95. Developed by the McDonnell Douglas Corporation before it was acquired by Boeing in 1996, the MD-95 was a derivative of the MD-90, and traced its roots back to the Douglas DC-9, which first flew in 1966.

While many of aviation history's important prototype aircraft have been cut up for scrap, the 367-80

The first and the last. Seen here on the Boeing Field ramp in September 1992 are the red and yellow Boeing 707 prototype (originally designated 367-80), which first flew in 1954, and the last 707 airframe, which was first flown 38 years later. The latter aircraft, delivered to the U.S. Navy as an E-6A electronic communications aircraft, marked the end of one of the greatest chapters in aviation history. The former aircraft was subsequently put on permanent display by the Smithsonian Institution's national Air & Space museum. *Manufacturer photo via the collection of Bill Yenne*

Dash-Eighty survived to serve Boeing for 18 years as a flight test aircraft. During that time, it flew with a fifth engine mounted on the aft fuselage to test installation feasibility of such a configuration on the Boeing 727. It flew with three different types of engines installed at the same time. It investigated engine-thrust reversers, engine sound suppressors, rigs designed to cause in-flight engine icing conditions, air conditioners, and wing flap and slat modifications. It was also used to test radar and radar antennas and even different paints. In one test series for landing gear, the aircraft was outfitted with oversized tires, and it landed and took off from muddy fields barely able to support the weight of passenger automobiles.

The 367-80 also flew special landing-approach studies at Moffett Field, California, for the National Aeronautics and Space Administration. A high-lift, slow-speed system featuring special wing flaps for direct-lift control was used in steeper-than-usual landing approaches designed to alleviate aircraft noise problems in residential areas near airports.

The Dash-Eighty was officially turned over to the Smithsonian Institution's National Air & Space Museum in May 1972, but it remained in storage in Arizona until May 1990, when Boeing returned the airplane to Seattle for a full restoration. The refurbished Dash-Eighty made a special fly-over of the Boeing facilities in Seattle and the Puget Sound area on July 15, 1991, to commemorate the 75th anniversary of the Boeing Company and the 37th anniversary of its own first flight. For several years thereafter, the aircraft remained on display at Boeing Field in Seattle.

Of the 878 commercial Model 707/720 variants, 138 were 707-120s, 5 were delivered as 707-220s before the designation change, 153 were 720-000s, 69 were basic 707-320s, 170 were 707-320Bs, 306 were 707-320Cs, and 37 were Rolls-Royce–powered 707-420 series aircraft.

The legacy of the Model 707 can still be seen in subsequent members of the Boeing jetliner family. Among these, the Models 727, 737, and 757 all have cabins with the same width and same basic design. In addition, the original Model 727 and 737 flight decks were based directly on that of the Model 707.

Excluding military variants, the Model 707/720 program eclipsed the Douglas DC-3 as the most successful airliner program in history, although several jetliners introduced after it have exceeded its production record. In terms of its impact on aviation history, however, it remains as one of the most important aircraft ever.

CHAPTER NINE

THE DC-8:

Douglas Enters the Jet Age

For more than two decades, the Douglas Aircraft Company was the foremost maker of airliners in the world. From the 1930s until the 1950s, the Douglas DC-3s, and later the DC-4s, DC-6s, and DC-7s, were ubiquitous on the airways of the United States and the world. Almost any flight line photograph of a major American airport taken during that time will show that Douglas equipment outnumbers that of any other planemaker. Among four-engine propliners, the only serious challenge came from Lockheed's Constellation.

In July 1954, when Boeing first flew its Model 367-80 jetliner prototype, Douglas was considering an advanced DC-7 or, like Lockheed, a turboprop airliner. Having witnessed the commercial failure of de Havilland's Comet, Douglas was understandably leery of leaping into an unknown field when it was so firmly in control of the airliner market.

It was not until June 1955 that Douglas formally announced that it would develop a turbojet powered airliner in the same size and weight class as the Boeing 707-120. By now, it was widely believed in the industry that the first jetliner in service would take the bulk of future orders. Boeing and Douglas were in a race to be first.

The DC-8 would be similar to the 707 in many ways. The two types would be within a few feet of having the same dimensions and passenger capacity. Both offered six-abreast seating and both had four turbojet engines mounted on underwing pylons for ease of maintenance. Both had swept wings, although the DC-8's were swept at 30 degrees, compared to 35 degrees on the 707, which gave it better slow-speed handling characteristics.

The DC-8 obviously offered an amazing improvement in performance over the Douglas DC-7. The jetliner would be more than half again faster and could carry nearly twice as many passengers. The DC-8 was designed to carry 118 people in an all-first-class configuration, or as many as 176 in its maximum-density format.

The initial DC-8-10 model series had a wingspan of 142 feet 5 inches and a wing area of 2,883 square feet. It was 150 feet 6 inches long and had a tail height of 42 feet 4 inches. It weighed 355,000 pounds fully loaded and fueled, and had a service ceiling of 35,000 feet.

The first DC-8-10 made its maiden flight from Long Beach Municipal Airport on Memorial Day, May 30, 1958—five months after the Boeing 707-120 made its initial flight. The takeoff weight for the first flight was 198,000 pounds, and the aircraft was powered by for 13,500-

A Douglas DC-8-62 in the colorful markings of Braniff International Airways. The brilliant livery designed by the abstract artist Alexander Calder were one of Braniff's more notable publicity efforts.

Clipper Flying Cloud, a Douglas DC-8-32, was delivered to Pan American in 1961 but transferred the following year to Panair do Brasil.

A Douglas DC-8-53 originally delivered to Northwest Airlines in 1960. Northwest's first DC-8 acquisition was a group of five DC-8-32s.

pound-thrust Pratt & Whitney JT3C-6s, the same turbojet engine chosen by Boeing for the Model 707-120.

An estimated 95,000 people watched from nearby vantage points as the big plane raced down a newly extended 10,000-foot runway and climbed out over the ocean. In the cockpit for the first flight were Douglas Chief Test Pilot A. G. "Heimie" Heimerdinger, Bill Magruder as copilot, Paul Patton at the flight engineer's station, and Bob Rizer, flight-test engineer. After a takeoff roll of only 3,250 feet, the crew put the DC-8 through initial low-altitude handling tests, then took it to a speed of 350 knots and an altitude of 21,000 feet before landing at Edwards AFB in the California desert, which would be the site of the ensuing flight test program.

Soon, Douglas had nine aircraft involved in the test program so that the various aspects of testing required for certification could be checked as quickly as possible. Meanwhile, in early 1956, Douglas had already commissioned the Link Aviation Company to build a "total test flight simulator," a forerunner to the simulators in routine use today, so that DC-8 pilots could receive a great deal of DC-8 cockpit training before they actually set foot in a real DC-8. Because they could start their training without actually having

to take up space in one of the real DC-8s, Douglas could train a larger number of pilots faster. The Link firm was best known for the famous Link "trainer" of World War II, a crude, ground-based system that gave pilot trainees the basics of flying before they climbed into a real cockpit. The DC-8 simulator was used by people who were already trained airline pilots, but who were unfamiliar with the DC-8 cockpit or its handling characteristics. After a stint in the simulator, they entered the cockpit already having a "feel" for the new jetliner.

Another aspect of DC-8 flight testing, which was aimed at giving potential customers more choices, was to test and certify the DC-8 with more than one engine type. In addition to the Pratt & Whitney JT3C-6, the JT4A series was also certified, as well as the British-made Rolls-Royce Conway R0012, which was a selling point for British Commonwealth customers.

While Pan American World Airways and American Airlines had been the launch customers for the Boeing project, Delta Air Lines and United Air Lines led the order book for the first Douglas jetliner. The first commercial delivery was to United on June 3, 1959, and the DC-8-10 series went into service with both Delta and United on September 18, 1959. This

The third Douglas DC-8-11 delivered to United Air Lines in flight over San Francisco Bay. The look of the San Francisco skyline dates the picture to the early 1960s.

was 11 months after the 707-120 had entered service with Pan American and a month after the 707-320 began operations. Over the coming years, many airlines, including Pan American, would be customers for both the Boeing and Douglas jetliners. The DC-8-10 series would include the DC-8-10 prototype, as well as 23 delivered as DC-8-11 and five as DC-8-12.

The DC-8-10 series, which became the basic model for domestic operations within the United States, was followed by the higher-performance DC-8-20, 34 of which were delivered as DC-8-21s. This variant, which first flew on November 29, 1958, was powered by four JT4A-9s, each rated at 16,800 pounds of thrust.

The Douglas response to the longer-range Boeing 707-320 would be the DC-8-30 and DC-8-40, intercontinental versions with increased fuel capacity. The DC-8-30 first flew on February 20, 1959, three months after the DC-8-20, powered by four JT4A-11s, each delivering 17,500 pounds of thrust. The Rolls-Royce Conway powered the DC-8-40, which first flew on July 23, 1959. Its rating was the same as that of the JT4A-11.

The range data of the respective model series would be 4,773 miles for the DC-8-10 series; 5,043 miles for the DC-8-20 series; 6,273 miles for the

A Douglas DC-8-31 in the markings of Pan American Grace (Panagra), a sister company of Pan American World Airways. Formed in 1929 as a joint venture of Pan American and the W.R. Grace shipping company, Panagra and its DC-8 fleet were acquired by Braniff in 1967.

Left

The Douglas DC-8 assembly line at Long Beach, California, during the 1960s—with aircraft destined for Swissair, Flying Tigers, United Air Lines, Air Canada, and Japan Airlines. The DC-9 line can be seen in the background.

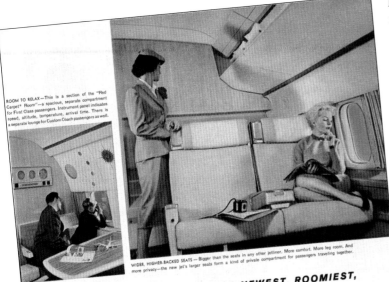

ONLY ON UNITED AIR LINES—THE NEWEST, ROOMIEST, BEST OF THE JETS—THE GREAT DC-8 JET MAINLINER

UNITED AIR LINES DC-8 JET MAINLINER BY DOUGLAS

THE BEST OF THE JETS...PLUS UNITED'S EXTRA CARE

When it first introduced the DC-8-11 in September 1959, United Air Lines described the Douglas jetliner as being the "newest." This was to distinguish it from the Boeing 707, which was already in service.

DC-8-30 series; and 6,756 miles for the DC-8-40 series. The figures for the latter two exceeded that of the Boeing 707-320 Intercontinental, which would enter service in August 1959.

The first DC-8-20 was delivered to Eastern Airlines on January 3, 1960. Just over a month later, on February 7, the first of both the DC-8-30 and DC-8-40 series were delivered in joint ceremonies to Pan American and to Air Canada, respectively. The longer range of the latter models was especially attractive to airlines such as Pan American and Air Canada with their long international routes. Pan American would also acquire DC-8-30 series aircraft for its Panagra (Pan American Grace) sister company in South America.

Alitalia, Italy's national flag carrier, was one of the first international customers for the DC-8, and one of its fleet made history on January 4, 1964, when Pope Paul VI became the first Roman Catholic pontiff to travel by air on an official visit. The pope's trip to Amman, Jordan, on that date would be only the first of many flights, including to the United States, that he would make as pope. Pius XII, who had been pope from 1939 to 1958, had traveled by air during a visit to the United States—as Cardinal Secretary of State Eugenio Pacelli—before becoming pope, but he had not made any official international trips by air during his papacy, nor had his successor, John XXIII.

While Douglas marketed the two types with the omnibus designations "DC-8-30" and "DC-8-40," the actual aircraft were produced in two series under six separate designations ending in the suffixes 31, 32, 33,

41, 42, and 43. The subvariants of the two series were distinguished by various detail differences as requested by specific customers.

The first turbofan-powered DC-8 would be the fifth variant, the DC-8-50, which was first flown on December 20, 1960. Entering service with the national flag carrier of the Netherlands, Koninklijke Luchtvaart Maatschappij (KLM, Royal Dutch Airlines) on April 3, 1961, it had four 18,000-pound-thrust Pratt & Whitney JT3D-3 turbofan engines, similar to those which Boeing offered on the Model 707-320B. The JT3D-3s also offered the efficiency to help boost the range of the DC-8-50 to 7,538 miles.

Douglas also produced a convertible passenger/cargo aircraft series with a 140 x 85-inch upward-hinged cargo door on the left side of the forward fuselage and reinforced floor under the designation DC-8-50CF. There was also a DC-8-50AF "all-freighter" version without cabin windows and provisions for passengers, such as galleys. During the 1970s, a number of earlier model DC-8s were re-engined with JT3Ds and redesignated as DC-8-50 series aircraft. Some of these, as well as some factory-delivered DC-8-50s, were retrofitted as convertible freighters and redesignated as DC-8-50CFs.

Again, as had been the case with "DC-8-30" and "DC-8-40," there was no actual "DC-8-50" aircraft, but rather they were produced under seven separate designations ending in the suffixes 51, 52, 53, 54AF, 54CF, 55, and 55CF.

The engines types may have changed, but the first five production series DC-8s—DC-8-10 through DC-8-50—all had the same dimensions as the original prototype. In 1966, though, the larger, longer-legged "Super Sixty" series DC-8s were introduced. Until this time, the Boeing Model 707, with nearly a year's head start in the marketplace, had emerged as the dominant jetliner, outselling the DC-8 two-to-one. The Super Sixty series was an effort by Douglas to reassert itself with an aircraft whose performance could match or exceed that of the competition.

The Super Sixty series included three subvariants, each of which was a different size, but all of which were larger than the previous DC-8s. The DC-8-61 and DC-8-63 were "stretched" by the insertion of additional fuselage sections fore and aft of the wings, increasing their length—by 37 feet over the earlier aircraft—to 187 feet 5 inches. The DC-8-62 was also "stretched," but only to 157 feet 5 inches. The DC-8-61 had the same wingspan as the earlier DC-8s, but the DC-8-62 and DC-8-63 had their wings enlarged 6

One of 11 Douglas DC-8-40 series aircraft operated by Air Canada. Formed in 1937 as Trans-Canada Airways, Canada's largest carrier had adopted the name Air Canada in 1964.

A Douglas DC-8-21 in the markings of Aeronaves de Mexico. The largest airline in Mexico became AeroMexico in 1972 and would buy six DC-8-50 series aircraft from Douglas.

feet to a span of 148 feet 5 inches. The DC-8-61CF had a cargo volume of 12,535 cubic feet.

The DC-8-61 and DC-8-63 could carry up to 259 passengers, more than any previous DC liner, while the DC-8-62 accommodated 189 travelers, and could fly farther than 7,700 miles, a range that exceeded that of any other DC liner to date. The concept of "Design for Growth" was a Douglas standard that had been represented as early as the transition from the DC-2 to the DC-3, and it occurred again with the evolution of the DC-4 to DC-7. However, it became especially manifest in the development of the DC-8-60 program, and in the subsequent DC-9 program.

The DC-8-61 was powered by the same JT3D-3 turbofan as the DC-8-50, but the DC-8-62 and DC-8-63 would have the JT3D-7, which delivered 19,000 pounds of thrust.

The DC-8-61 made its first flight on March 14, 1966, followed by the first DC-8-62 on August 29. The first commercial delivery of a DC-8-61 was to United Air Lines on January 26, 1967, and the first for the DC-8-62 was to the Scandinavian Airlines System (SAS) on May 3. On June 16, 1968, Japan Airlines would inaugurate nonstop service between Tokyo and San Francisco with the DC-8-62, helping to demonstrate the extremely long legs of the aircraft.

This phase of the DC-8 evolution occurred against the backdrop of major changes that were occurring within the Douglas Aircraft Company. By 1966, Douglas had begun to experience a financial crisis that put its corporate survival in jeopardy. The problems were not born of a lack of business—Douglas had a substantial backlog of orders—but rather from the staggering cost of gearing up for

that business. This was combined with severe inflation and shortages of labor and materials, both of which had resulted from a recession and the Vietnam War. Douglas had alleviated its cash flow difficulties with short-term financing, but the company needed a long-term loan and this was simply not available.

Against this backdrop, the Douglas board of directors voted to send out bid invitations to possible merger prospects. These included the other Southern California aerospace giants—North American Aviation, the Lockheed Corporation, and General Dynamics' Convair Division—as well as the Chrysler Corporation and Garrett, a Los Angeles aerospace systems company that had merged with the Signal Oil Company in 1964. Even billionaire Howard Hughes was planning to put in an offer. Another suitor was the McDonnell Aircraft Company of St. Louis, whose chairman, James Smith McDonnell, had been interested in working with Douglas since as early as 1959, when there were discussions about a joint venture in the field of small commercial aircraft.

When Douglas sent out a request for proposals, McDonnell seized the opportunity. He submitted the boldest, and, as it turned out, the winning bid. On January 13, 1967, a deal was struck, and on April 28, the merger between McDonnell and Douglas was finalized and the McDonnell Douglas Corporation became a reality.

The 75-year-old Douglas founder, Donald Wills Douglas, retired from active participation in company affairs but remained as honorary chairman of the board of directors, a title he held until his death in 1981. Meanwhile, 68-year-old James Smith McDonnell served as chairman and chief executive officer of

the new McDonnell Douglas Corporation until his death in August 1980.

Officially the "first McDonnell Douglas jetliner," the DC-8-63, made its debut on April 10, 1967, followed by an initial airline delivery to KLM on July 15. All of the design improvements of the DC-8-61 and DC-8-62 had been incorporated into the DC-8-63, including the fuselage extension, aerodynamic improvements to nacelles, pylons, and flaps, plus the increased wingspan and fuel capacity. These combined to provide its greatly increased payload and range capability. The final factory-built DC-8 variant was the DC-8-63CF convertible freighter, which made its first flight on March 18, 1968, and saw its first airline delivery two months later on June 21 to Seaboard World Airlines. The DC-8-63CF was able to carry up to 118,000 pounds of freight, accommodating 18 standard cargo pallets in the main cabin.

On May 13, 1972, after 15 years of production, the last of 556 DC-8 series aircraft was delivered. At that time, there were 48 DC-8 operators in 28 nations. United Air Lines, one of the two launch customers

and the original airline customer to have operated the largest fleet, maintained DC-8s in regularly scheduled service until October 31, 1991.

Of the total number of DC-8s produced, nearly half (262) were of the DC-8-60 Super Sixty series. This included 78 DC-8-61s; 10 DC-8-61CFs; 51 DC-8-62s; 6 DC-8-AFs; 10 DC-8-62Fs; 41 DC-8-63s; 7 DC-8-63AFs; 53 DC-8-63CFs; and 6 DC-8-63PFs.

Second to the Super Sixty series were the 142 DC-8-50s, which included 30 DC-8-51s; 25 DC-8-52s; 25 DC-8-53s; 15 DC-8-54AFs; 15 DC-8-54CFs; 8 DC-8-55s; and 24 DC-8-55CFs.

The 152 early preturbofan DC-8s included the original DC-8-10 prototype; 23 DC-8-11s; 5 DC-8-12s; 34 DC-8-21s; 4 DC-8-31s; 42 DC-8-32s; 11 DC-8-33s; 4 DC-8-41s; 8 DC-8-42s; and 20 DC-8-43s.

The largest DC-8 customer was launch customer United Air Lines with a total of 104 aircraft. These included 21 DC-8-10s (17 DC-8-11s and 5 DC-8-12s), 14 DC-8-21s, 13 DC-8-52s, 15 DC-8-54AF freighters, 30 DC-8-61s, and 10 DC-8-62s. Delta, the other launch customer, would acquire 6 DC-8-11s, 14 DC-8-51s, and 10 DC-8-61s.

A Douglas DC-8-63 in the livery of Eastern Airlines. An early DC-8 customer, Eastern had helped launch the DC-8-20 series, and it bought a total of 19 "Super Sixty" aircraft.

As Douglas employees worked round-the-clock in the late 1960s, DC-8 aircraft were rolling off the Douglas assembly line at Long Beach, California. By this time, a huge backlog of orders at Long Beach was pushing Douglas behind schedule and toward bankruptcy.

A Douglas DC-8-63 in the livery of Philippine Airlines. The pair of DC-8-63s that the Philippine flag carrier ordered had been preceded by a single DC-8-55.

Eastern Airlines, whose early order for 15 DC-8-21s had been an important program milestone, would buy a total of 35, including a DC-8-51, 13 DC-8-61s, and 6 DC-8-63 freighters.

Pan American, which had actually bought the first 25 of the DC-8 serial numbers under the DC-8-31 designation, placed no further orders for DC-8s for its own use, but bought a single DC-8-55CF for Panagra before the latter was taken over by Braniff. In turn, Braniff bought 5 DC-8-62s for the former Panagra operations in South America. Braniff also, subsequently, bought two more DC-8-62s. Other American passenger carrier customers included Capital and National, while Airlift, Atlantis, Flying Tigers, Seaboard World, and Universal were major customers for the freighter variants.

Air Canada, which launched the DC-8-40 series, acquired 7 such aircraft, as well as 3 DC-8-53s, 6 DC-8-54CFs, 6 DC-8-61s, and 13 DC-8-63s. KLM, which launched the DC-8-50 series, as well as the DC-8-63,

bought 9 of the former and 7 of the latter (including a pair of DC-8-55CF convertible freighters), but these were preceded by 7 DC-8-32s. SAS, which launched the DC-8-62, acquired 7 of them, as well as an equal number of DC-8-32s, a pair of DC-8-55s, and 3 DC-8-63s. Japan Airlines acquired 8 DC-8-30 series, 6 DC-8-50 series, 7 DC-8-61s, and 13 DC-8-62s.

Other foreign commercial customers included Aeromexico, Air New Zealand, Air Afrique, Air Zaire, Alitalia, Canadian Pacific, France's UTA, Finnair of Finland, Garuda of Indonesia, Iberia of Spain, Pakistan Air Lines, Swissair, Trans Caribbean, and VIASA of Venezuela. France's Armee de l'Air was the only

military customer that Douglas had for the entire DC-8 program, and they bought a single DC-8-55CF.

Beginning in 1981, many of the Super Sixty series DC-8 aircraft still in service were re-engined with new technology General Electric/SNECMA (Société National d'Etudes et Construction de Moteurs d'Avion) high-bypass turbofan engines. These aircraft were then redesignated, with the DC-8-61 becoming the DC-8-71, and so on through the DC-8-72 and DC-8-73. These became known as the "Super *Seventy*" series. The DC-8-70 series aircraft would retain the DC-8-60 series operating weights, but provided customers with a longer range because of the newer,

A color view of a Douglas DC-8-62 originally sold to Braniff in 1969 but later operated by Arrow Air and Rich International. The "Super Sixty" DC-8s have had a full life in the after market.

One of ten Douglas DC-8-21s ordered by United Air Lines during its initial round of DC-8 series acquisition. That first round saw United buying a total of 30 DC-8s of various types.

October 17, 1959

Delta DC-8 Royal Jet Service is for Everybody

Deluxe First Class and Thrifty Supercoach

Passengers on Delta's initial DC-8 Royal Jet Service flights between Atlanta and New York will be quick to recognize that a new standard of luxury and comfort has been established in this swift moving Jet Age.

World's newest, largest true jetliner, the DC-8 is years ahead in design and decor. Quiet, vibration-free cabins of new beauty and spaciousness feature the accommodations for both first class and supercoach passengers. Cruising at nearly 600 mph, these luxurious jetliners provide a host of new conveniences and substantially more individual room for all passengers. Inaugural service over routes shown on the map will be effective:

Atlanta-New York, now operating   Chicago-Miami, Atlanta-Miami, October 15   Remainder of pattern to late November

Reservations now being accepted on all routes

DELTA AIR LINES

Initial Delta DC-8 Royal Jet Service Routes

DETROIT   NEW YORK

CHICAGO

DALLAS   ATLANTA

NEW ORLEANS

MIAMI

DELTA DC-8 JETLINER

more fuel-efficient turbofans. The Super Seventy series was officially certified in 1982.

The 4,600-pound CFM56-2 engine used for the DC-8-70 series delivered 22,000 pounds of thrust in a sea level takeoff, but, because of it, the Super Seventy series aircraft were also able to meet the more stringent noise regulations that were mandated by the U.S. Federal Aviation Administration during the 1980s.

It should be noted that not all of the Super Sixty Series were retrofitted with CFM56-2 engines to become Super Seventy aircraft.

Also during the 1980s, McDonnell Douglas undertook an extensive program of converting passenger DC-8s, especially Super Sixty series aircraft, to freighter configuration, by cutting cargo doors and installing strengthened main deck flooring.

On June 1, 1998, the DC-8 marked the 40th anniversary of its first flight with a fleet record of nearly 30 million hours of revenue service. The DC-8 had been born as a Douglas airplane and ended production as a McDonnell Douglas airplane. In a twist of several ironies, the 40th anniversary of the first

Douglas jetliner occurred a year-and-a-half after the McDonnell Douglas Corporation itself had ceased to exist. In December 1996, it had been absorbed into the Boeing Company, whose Model 707 had been the foil against which the DC-8 had competed during the early years of the jetliner era.

At the time of the DC-8's 40th anniversary, 294 of the original 556 aircraft still remained in service with 50 operators around the world. The majority of these aircraft were freighters and freighter conversions operated by the air express industry. The largest single operator at the turn of the century

was United Parcel Service, with a fleet of 49 DC-8-71 and DC-8-73 freighters. Other major airlines flying the aircraft included Emery Worldwide, with a fleet of 40 DC-8-60s and DC-8-70s; Airborne Express, with 35 DC-8-60 series aircraft; and Air Transport International, with 25 DC-8-60 and DC-8-70 series aircraft.

Having flown more than 13.8 billion statute miles and carried more than 950 million passengers, the DC-8 family was flying more than 270 scheduled passenger flights daily to 140 cities in 58 countries at the turn of the century.

A Douglas DC-8-63CF convertible freighter in the livery of Overseas National Airways (ONA). Formed as a charter carrier during the Korean War, ONA became a DC-8 operator in 1966.

CHAPTER TEN

THE 880/990 SERIES:

Too Much, Too Late

onvair reached the jet age as one of world's leading aircraft manufacturers. Its World War II military aircraft were legendary, and its postwar military aircraft were also extremely important. Its family of Model 240, 340, and 440 Convairliners had been one of the most successful families of twin-engine propliners produced anywhere in the world. Produced from the late 1940s through the mid-1950s, they were successful both in airline service and as a product line for their manufacturer. They were reliable and efficient, and they were popular with both the airlines and their passengers. Meanwhile, Convair's jet credentials were equally respectable. The company's B-58 Hustler was the first supersonic strategic bomber to go into service, and its F-102 and F-106 jet interceptors were the backbone of the U.S. Air Force Air (later Aerospace) Defense Command.

It seemed in the late 1950s that such a company would be a strong contender in the jetliner field. However, both Boeing and Douglas already had four-engine jetliners entering service when Convair decided to develop a new aircraft that would compete directly with their 707 and DC-8 aircraft.

Convair's fateful decision to enter the world of four-engine jetliners was spurred in large part by a specific order from Howard Hughes, the eccentric billionaire and aviation enthusiast who owned 78 percent of the stock in TransWorld Airlines (TWA), a company that he had controlled since before World War II. Had it not been for Hughes, Convair's planners may have thought twice about allowing the company to become the third entry in the competitive and overcrowded market for four-engine jetliners.

In about 1954, Convair had considered designing a small, twin-jet aircraft to serve the same market as the Convairliners, but the project was shelved. The eyes of the airlines were on the big jets for transcontinental and transoceanic service. A decade later, when Boeing introduced the 737 and Douglas the DC-9, it quickly became obvious that there was a market for both long- *and* short-range jetliners. Convair had had the chance to continue in a market that it already dominated—but they had already lost an opportunity that would not recur for them.

In April 1956, with Hughes having dangled the carrot of a big order for Convair jetliners, the company formally announced that it was going to develop a jetliner similar to the 707 and DC-8 that would be powered by four commercial variants of the General Electric CJ-805-3, the civilian version of the J79 turbojets that the company was using for the B-58 Hustler.

In January 1962, Swissair was the second customer to receive its Convair 990s, but on March 9 of that year, it would become the first airline to put the type into service. Initial service was to the Far East.

The fourth Convair 880, produced for Delta Air Lines but seen here at Anchorage International Airport in company livery during cold weather tests, circa 1959.

The new jetliner was named "Skylark," and, by picking the next available model number, it was designated as Convair Model 22. This was later changed to "Model 600" to reflect the speed of the aircraft in miles per hour. None of these appellations suited Howard Hughes, so they had to change. The impulsive Hughes had decided that his new jetliner should be called "Golden Arrow," and that it should be manufactured of solid gold!

Making an airplane out of solid gold was, of course, impossible. When this inconvenient fact was explained to Hughes, he requested that all of the aluminum panels be anodized, or plated with gold. Tests were done, and it was determined that the plating could not be done uniformly, so the result would be an airplane that looked like it was covered with a quilt. When Hughes saw that he couldn't get the desired result from the anodizing, he abandoned the whole idea. The Golden Arrow was once again the Skylark, although the name was rarely used.

The Model 600 designation was also abandoned, and the number was reapplied to the turboprop Convairliner conversion. On the engineering record books, the "Model 22" designation was retained for the new jetliner, but "880" ultimately became the official *name* of the aircraft.

There are a variety of stories about the reasons for the origin of the "880," but none of them is definitive. Two versions of the tale have been circulated as "official." One was that the jetliner was twice as big, with twice the performance of the Model 440. Another is that the number was based on its cruising speed of 880 feet per second, a clever way of demonstrating the importance of speed in the new world of jet air travel. Indeed, the 880 was to be the fastest of the first-generation jetliners, as it would be powered by same engine that powered the supersonic B-58.

Another explanation was that the aircraft would be delivered in a luxury configuration, and carry 88 first class passengers four abreast in 22 rows. The best story, vouched for by Jack Zevely, Convair's vice president for sales, was that Convair had been through 880 meetings with Hughes and his staff before the contract was finally signed.

Howard Hughes committed to 30 aircraft for TWA (designated as Model 22-1), and Delta ordered 10 (designated as Model 22-2) before Hughes demanded that no more be sold to U.S. carriers who might compete with him.

The Convair 880 had a wingspan of 120 feet and a wing area of 2,000 square feet. It was 129 feet 4 inches long and had a tail height of 36 feet 4 inches. The Boeing 707-120 had a wingspan of 130 feet 10 inches, a wing area of 2,433 square feet, and was 145 feet 1 inch long. The Douglas DC-8 had a wingspan of 142 feet 5 inches and was 150 feet 6 inches long.

Although the 880 would be in the same size and weight class as the 707 and DC-8, the decision to design it around four-abreast first class seating resulted in a narrower fuselage. This meant that when the aircraft was later adapted for mixed class seating, the fuselage width would force a five-abreast seating arrangement rather than the six-abreast layout offered by the others. This meant that it could accommodate fewer ticket-buying passengers.

The first 880 flew from San Diego's Lindbergh Field on January 27 (some sources say January 29), 1959, with Convair test pilots Phil Prophett and Don Germeraad at the controls. After flight testing—which included the near-disaster of a vertical stabilizer shredding in flight—the first 880 configured for actual passenger use was completed in August 1959. By the end of the year, the aircraft were starting to roll off the assembly line.

In the meantime, a crisis was brewing within TWA as Howard Hughes battled with management for control of the airline. Hughes may have been the majority stockholder, but he held no actual management position with the airline, nor did he have the confidence of the consortium of banks and other institutions that underwrote TWA's line of credit.

TWA was supposed to take delivery of the first three 880s, but Hughes stalled on acceptance, so Delta was the first to put the aircraft into service. On its delivery flight on February 10, 1960, the first Delta 880 set a transcontinental speed record, flying from San Diego to Miami in three hours and 31 minutes. Delta's first scheduled, revenue-producing flight left New York for Houston on the morning of May 1, 1960.

Meanwhile, things were not going well for Howard Hughes. On March 5, 1960, the TWA credit line was severed by its lenders, with the airline $125 million in debt. For Convair, the situation was critical because the deal it had made with Hughes had called for a balloon payment on delivery, rather than progress payments. This meant that TWA could delay paying for its 30 880s if it did not accept delivery. Hughes even took the unprecedented step of seizing the first three 880s off the factory floor, pulling them across the tarmac away from Convair property, and surrounding them with armed guards. At first, Hughes even tried to prevent Delta from picking up its own 880s by insisting that his contract stated that TWA should be the first to fly its aircraft. On this

The first Convair 880 flight test aircraft on the runway at San Diego's Lindbergh Field, where Phil Prophett and Don Germeraad began the flight test program in January 1959.

Alaska Airlines' fifth Convair 880 was the 54th aircraft in the program, and the 10th modified 880M. The carrier had previously operated Convairliners, so naturally it was interested in Convair jets. Alaska used 880s only briefly, opting for Boeing and McDonnell Douglas equipment.

point, at least, he was compelled to back down. However, Convair had to put 13 partially or nearly completed 880s into storage until 1961, and this placed a heavy financial burden on the company. They too had to borrow heavily to keep going.

A new financial package for TWA was finally negotiated, but the deal prevented Hughes from meddling in the day-to-day affairs of the company. On December 15, 1960, the new loans were released to TWA, and the 78 percent of the stock owned by Hughes was placed in a 10 year trust. He had lost control of "his" airline, and the first TWA 880 was finally delivered in January 1961.

Meanwhile, Convair had announced the "Modified" 880M, which would be powered by four General Electric CJ-805-3B turbojets, each rated at 11,650 pounds of thrust. The 880M had a cruising speed of 556 miles per hour at 35,000 feet and a top speed of 586.5 miles per hour at 22,500 feet. It had a ceiling of 41,000 feet and a range of 4,050 miles. This higher gross weight variant weighed 93,000 pounds empty and had a gross of 193,500. The 880M configuration was first flown on October 3, 1960, and first entered service with Civil Air Transport of the Republic of

An interesting, albeit posed, period view of the first-class lounge of a Convair 880, circa 1959. These ladies dressed as though flying first class was a formal affair. Note that smoking was not only permissible, but cigarettes were provided.

Cathay Pacific's first Convair 880M was the first order in the program from a non-U.S. air carrier to be delivered. Originally formed in Hong Kong in 1946 to operate passenger flights to Manila, Bangkok, Singapore, and Shanghai, the carrier grew at an average rate of 20 percent a year between 1962 and 1967.

China (Taiwan) in 1961 under the designation Model 22-4. Subsequent orders were placed by Alaska Airlines as Model 22-21, VIASA of Venezuela as Model 22-3, and Japan Airlines as Model 22-22.

Convair's tardiness in entering the jetliner field, combined with the production delays and the Hughes interference, meant that the 880 series was not the success for which the company had hoped. The idea of adapting the J79 engine for commercial use was also costly. It was a temperamental, high-maintenance engine, and it proved to be very fuel inefficient. Unfortunately, the aircraft had been designed around the engine and retrofitting another powerplant was discovered to be impractical.

Convair had needed to sell at least 120 aircraft in order to offset development costs and turn a profit, but only 65 880s were built, including 17 880Ms.

Only 27 of the 30 880s on TWA's original order were delivered, and several of these were leased to Northeast Airlines, a regional carrier. Those that did remain with TWA served only for a few years, mainly on routes within the continental United States such as between Kansas City and Los Angeles. The last TWA 880 was retired in June 1974.

Before its acquisition by Delta Air Lines in 1972, Northeast Airlines operated nine Convair 880s. Five of these were part of the original TWA order and were later re-registered from Northeast to TWA, two were originally registered to TWA and later leased to Northeast, and two were registered to Northeast directly.

Delta, the first airline to operate a Convair jetliner, bought a total of 17 880s, including the 65th and last aircraft. However, because of the lack of fuel efficiency, Delta took all of the 880s out of service in 1973, the first year of the energy crisis. One of the Delta 880s was sold to the King of Rock and Roll, Elvis Presley, who named it *Lisa Marie* after his daughter and used it to fly to his concerts. After his death in 1977, it was placed on permanent display across the street from his Graceland estate in Memphis, Tennessee.

Swissair, a long-time customer for Convair propliners, would own several 880s, but not as its first choice. Switzerland's national carrier had actually wanted to wait for the 880's successor, the 990, and had ordered nine of these in partnership with the Scandinavian Airlines System (SAS). Meanwhile, Capital Airlines of the United States had cancelled an order for seven 880Ms, and these were offered to Swissair as an interim substitute for the 990s. Swissair accepted the proposal for seven, but records show that

only two actually bore Swiss registry. Japan Airlines bought one of these from Swissair and six 880Ms directly from Convair. Hong Kong-based Cathay Pacific purchased seven 880Ms secondhand, including two from Japan Airlines, and one directly from Convair. Cathay Pacific would be the last of the original airline operators to keep the 880 in service, finally retiring the last one in 1975.

The unforeseen energy crisis of 1973–1974 had marked the end for the 880 as a practical jetliner. Despite its speed, the 880 was far less fuel efficient per passenger mile than its competitors. Nevertheless, secondhand 880s continued in service well into the 1980s, and the last aircraft was still being operated by NASA at the turn of the century.

Convair made the decision to go ahead with development of its second jetliner even before the first, the 880, had made its maiden flight. This new aircraft, designated as Model 30 but best known as the "Convair 990," was similar to and based upon the 880, but it was 10 feet and 1 inch longer, and it incorporated new engines.

In retrospect, the "990" appellation for the 880's successor is obvious, but in the beginning, Convair was afraid to use it. Howard Hughes, whose order for 880s had launched that program, demanded that any name chosen for the Model 30 should not appear to diminish the importance of "his" 880. To appease the eccentric Hughes, Convair assured him that they would resurrect the name "Convair 600." A lower number attached to a later airplane made little marketing sense, but Convair breathed easier when Hughes placed his own order for the new aircraft, and they were able to formally adopt the 990 number.

The fuselage stretch came in response to a need for increased passenger capacity in order to compete with the Douglas DC-8, the Boeing 707, and the

This 1958 magazine ad suggested that the Convair 990 was part of what Leonardo da Vinci imagined when he wrote his treatise on flight half a millennium before.

as-yet-untested Boeing 720 (707-220). However, the fuselage width would remain the same as the 880. This left the new aircraft with five-abreast seating rather than the six-abreast configuration offered by Douglas and Boeing. Passenger capacity ranged from 90 to 149, depending on configuration.

The Convair 990 had a wingspan of 120 feet, the same as the 880, and a wing area of 2,250 square feet, compared to the 2,000 square feet of the 880. It weighed 120,560 pounds empty and had a gross weight of 255,000 pounds. The engines originally chosen for the 990 were the General Electric CJ-805-21, a turbofan development of the CJ-805-3 turbojet that had been used on the 880. Ultimately, the CJ-805-23, a successor to the CJ-805-21, was actually installed.

The 990 had a cruising speed of 570 miles per hour at 35,000 feet and a maximum speed of 625 miles per hour at 21,200 feet. Its range with maximum payload was 3,800 miles, and its range with maximum fuel was 5,400 miles.

The first order for 25 of the new Model 30 was announced by American Airlines in 1958 even as the first 880 was still being built. In order to save time getting the aircraft into service, Convair made the

decision that the first aircraft would not be a prototype, but would be a Model 30-5 production aircraft that would actually go to American Airlines after Convair flight tests.

Time was critical, for while General Electric was developing its new turbofan, Pratt & Whitney was hurrying to get its competing JT-3D turbofan engine ready for Boeing's 720. As events unfolded, the JT-3D was ready sooner and the Boeing 720 would be in service two years ahead of the 990.

The improved performance of the new General Electric CJ-805-23 resulted in top speeds close to the sound barrier, but the resulting supersonic airflow across the wing resulted in extreme vibration and aerodynamic drag. To solve this problem, Convair worked with engineers at the National Advisory Committee for Aeronautics (NACA, the precursor of NASA) to develop the antishock structures known as "speed pods" that would be installed aft of the engines on the trailing edge of its wings. This gave the Model 30 a distinctive appearance that distinguished it from all other aircraft of its class.

The delays that were caused by the development of the engine and the need to redesign the 990's wing would be critical. The first Model 30 finally flew on January 24, 1961—almost exactly two years after the 880—with 880-veteran test pilot Don Germeraad as pilot. The first delivery to American Airlines would occur a year later. It should have been sooner, but the extensive flight test program revealed numerous aerodynamic flaws that had not shown up during wind tunnel tests. The changes needed to correct these problems consumed a great deal of overtime at the Convair engineering department and included such fixes as adding Krueger leading edge slats, moving the engine pylons 28 inches, and reshaping the engine nacelles.

With the time lost in the modification process, American's first 990 didn't actually go into scheduled service until March 18, 1962, by which time the original order for 25 aircraft had been reduced to 20.

Meanwhile, because of the delays, TWA cancelled the order for 13 aircraft that Howard Hughes had placed in November 1960, a month before he lost control of the airline. Hughes was so angry about the cancellation that his attorney, Chester Davis, actually

The *Lisa Marie* was a Convair 880, originally operated by Delta Air Lines, but best known as the personal aircraft of Elvis Presley. The King of Rock and Roll used it extensively during his exhausting tour schedule in the mid-1970s. After his death in August 1977, his estate put the aircraft on display near his former home at Graceland in Memphis, Tennessee.

proposed that the Hughes Tool Company would buy $11.2 million worth of TWA debentures if the airline would reinstate the order for 990s. The relationship between man and airline disintegrated into a nightmare of suit and countersuit. In 1963, TWA would prevail in their litigation after the reclusive billionaire refused to appear in court. Ultimately, Hughes sold his TWA shares in May 1966 for a staggering $546 million, which assured his standing as "the world's richest man."

Swissair, the second 990 customer to receive its aircraft, was actually the first to fly passengers, putting its aircraft to work between Europe and the Far East nine days ahead of the first American flight. The

This dramatic November 1960 view clearly shows the Convair 990's signature "speed pods" or "speed capsules" designed to minimize the sonic shock wave and its resultant drag.

The prototype Convair 990 on the runway at San Diego's Lindbergh Field, where flight testing began on January 24, 1961, almost exactly two years after that of the 880, and with the same test pilot, Don Germeraad.

Brazil's Redes Estaduais Aereas Limitada (REAL) was a customer for earlier Convair equipment, but the 990 aircraft ordered by REAL were actually delivered to Viacao Aerea do Rio Grande (Varig). This Christening scene took place with one of the series prototypes.

Swissair 990s were of the Model 30-6 type, having been optimized for long-range, over-water operations.

It was Swissair that first used the name "Coronado" for the 990, but the name was eventually used by most operators. The name had been used previously for the PB2Y flying boat built in the 1940s by Consolidated Aircraft Corporation before it merged with Vultee to form Convair. It was derived from the island in San Diego Bay—visible from the Convair factories at Lindbergh Field—that is still home to the San Diego Naval Base.

Swissair had originally ordered nine 990s (Model 30-6s) in partnership with Scandinavian Airlines System (SAS), but the latter dropped out

CONVAIR JET-LINER

CONVAIR JET-LINER
MASTERPIECE OF *Design*

Designed in every detail to lead the way, the new jet-age Los Angeles International
Airport and the Convair Jet-Liner will bring tomorrow's travel beyond your dreams.
For you, the jet-age traveler, both this airport and
the Convair 880 Jet-Liner are *Masterpieces of Design.*

CONVAIR

A DIVISION OF GENERAL DYNAMICS CORPORATION

Among airlines first to offer Convair 880 Jet-Liner service will be TWA, DELTA, TRANSCONTINENTAL (Argentina), REAL-AEROVIAS (Brazil)

This 1958 magazine ad stressed futuristic design and placed a streamlined artist's conception near the also futuristic new terminal at Los Angeles International Airport.

of the purchase deal and eventually just leased a pair of them from Swissair. Other customers included Garuda of Indonesia, which ordered three, and Varig in Brazil, which took over an order for three (designated Model 30-8) placed by REAL, another Brazilian carrier, and a long-time customer for the earlier Convair propliners. Garrett AiResearch and APSA of Costa Rica each bought one, bringing the total to 37 aircraft, a disappointing tally for Convair.

As with the 880, the 990 was a durable aircraft that was popular with crews but which suffered from poor fuel efficiency, which made it unpopular with the airlines, especially in the wake of the 1973–1974 energy crisis. As with the 880, it also had a lower passenger capacity than the competition, and this also compromised its sales potential.

American Airlines began to divest itself of its 990 fleet in 1965, even before Convair had shut down the San Diego assembly line. Swissair followed suit, selling its fleet to carriers such as Air Afrique, a multinational consortium in former French West Africa and Israel's El Al. All of the Swissair fleet were ultimately sold except one that was donated to the Transport Museum in Luzern. The national flag carrier of Indonesia, Garuda, bought three Convair 990s which remained in service into the 1970s. Most 990s would

continue in service for less than a decade, but the Spanish charter carrier, Spantax, which at one time operated a fleet of 14 of them, continued to fly at least 1 990 until 1987.

The 880/990 program was the financial disaster that put Convair out of the business of making airplanes. The cost of developing jetliner technology far exceeded the return that Convair got on a mere 102 880 and 990 airframes. Douglas would build more than five times as many DC-8s and Boeing would build nearly ten times as many 707s.

Except for a single Model 48 counter-insurgency aircraft flown in 1964, the 990 marked the end of aircraft building at Convair. It was the last Convair production aircraft and the last Convair jet. General Dynamics, Convair's parent corporation, retained missile production in San Diego but shifted new aircraft production to the General Dynamics facility at Fort Worth, which was originally a Convair plant. Convair's flagship San Diego factory—which had built over 12,000 aircraft since before World War II—became a subcontractor to such Fort Worth projects as the F-111 and the F-16. Ironically, from 1970 until the great San Diego factory was torn down in 1996, the Convair Division of General Dynamics built fuselage sections for the McDonnell Douglas DC-10 and MD-ll jetliners.

CHAPTER ELEVEN

THE 727:

Boeing Starts a Family

In the mid-1950s, Boeing and Douglas created their first jetliners to compete on the longest and highest density routes possible. It was where both the money and the media attention were. The Boeing 707 and Douglas DC-8 were specifically designed to fly as far or farther than the longest range propliners then in service. Among the competitors of the 707 and DC-8, both the British de Havilland Comet 4 and the American Convair 880 were also designed to compete for the glamorous, long-distance, high-profile routes.

Achieving routine service across the United States and across the North Atlantic were the primary goals of the first jetliners. The shorter, lower-density routes, such as within the United States and within Europe, were of secondary importance, and they continued to be served by propliners—for the time being.

However, sooner or later, the world's airlines would need a jet equivalent of the Douglas DC-3. The remarkable DC-3 had revolutionized air travel in the late 1930s, not by serving important major cities—although it did—but by bringing safe, reliable air transportation to many small and medium-size cities, and linking them to one another and to the outside world. The DC-3 was not famous for flying fast and far, although it certainly had respectable speed and range for its time, but for being ubiquitous. It had made air travel *available*.

What the world needed in the early 1960s was an aircraft that would make *jet* air travel available. Flying to Europe was exciting and glamorous, but the average business and vacation traveler wanted a safe and reliable airplane with turbojet speed that could fly into virtually any airport that had been served—and in many cases that *still* was being served—by the ubiquitous DC-3. In fact, the Model 727 would prove to be so versatile that it was the first jetliner ever certified for operations from a gravel runway.

The twin-jet French Sud-Aviation Caravelle, which first flew in 1955, was the first jetliner that was designed specifically for shorter routes. In retrospect, this was a revolutionary marketing concept, especially because it was one that the American manufacturers had not yet seriously considered. The idea of a jetliner replacement for short-range propliners remained a low priority with American planemakers. Boeing had responded with the Model 720, a smaller version of the 707, but it was still too large for most runways in most smaller airports. American planemakers had all done some preliminary design studies and had announced these studies at various points during the 1950s, but they had little to show for it until late in the decade.

An Air France 727-228 on her delivery flight over Mount St. Helens in southern Washington. Before the celebrated and catastrophic 1980 eruption of this presumed-to-be-dormant volcano, Mount St. Helens had been just another peak among the Cascades. After the eruption, it would temporarily replace Mount Rainier as a favorite background for Boeing in-flight photos.

Seen here circa 1972, *Clipper Golden Age* was a Boeing 727-021QC (Quick Change) that was originally sold to Pan American in 1966, but operated by Federal Express after Pan American folded in 1991.

The Sud-Aviation Caravelle entered service in May 1959, a month before the DC-8, and American planemakers took their wakeup call. In February 1960, Douglas licensed marketing rights to the Caravelle and even took an option on a license to build it in the United States. At the same time, though, the California planemaker pressed ahead with its own twinjet, the DC-9.

Boeing accelerated plans for a small jet of its own, and by December 5, 1960, it was able to announced the launch of the Model 727, with confirmed orders from United Air Lines and Eastern Airlines for 40 aircraft each. Both airlines would ultimately place additional orders, with United eventually buying 230 and Eastern a total of 163.

Like the Model 707, the Model 727 series would be built at Boeing's facility at Renton, Washington, located southeast of Seattle at the foot of Lake Washington. It was here that the first aircraft rolled out on November 27, 1962, to make its first flight on February 9, 1963. The aircraft was designed around the same fuselage as its sister ship, the 707, but it was distinguished by its high "T" tail and by having all of its engines clustered around the tail. Operators of the Caravelle had discovered that its rear-mounted engines provided a quieter cabin, so Boeing used this feature for the sake of sound damping and also to allow the wings to be more efficient by their being unencumbered with the aerodynamic drag of engines and their nacelles.

Although the intake of the center engine was located above the other two, the engine itself was located in line horizontally with the other two and connected to the intake by an "S-shaped" duct. Having all three engines adjacent to one another and at the same height from the ground facilitated maintenance for operators and was to be one of the Model 727's selling points.

Pioneered by the Caravelle, the noise-reducing properties of rear-mounted engines were used in three other small commercial transports that also made their debut in 1963. These were the British Aerospace BAC-111, the Soviet Tupolev Tu-134, and the Soviet Ilyushin Il-62. All of these aircraft also used the "T" tail configuration used by Boeing for the Model 727.

A fourth aircraft with a "T" tail and rear-mounted engines was the British Aerospace Trident, which was originally developed as the de Havilland DH-121. Making its first flight a year ahead of the Boeing 727, the Trident also had three engines and an "S-shaped" center intake duct. At first glance, it could be mistaken for a Boeing 727.

Boeing had originally considered using two engines, but the third was added for safety and because of restrictions (since lifted) on twin-engine aircraft operating on over-water routes. Actually the idea of three engines had been settled early in the design program, and placing one on each wing had been considered before the Boeing team settled on the rear fuselage configuration. Of the era's other "T-tailed small jetliners, the Il-62 had four, while the BAC-111 and Tu-134 had two each. The Tu-134 was later followed by the similar Tu-154, which had three engines. The Douglas DC-9, which would be introduced in 1965, would be another "T"-tailed, twin-engine, small jetliner.

The three engines that powered the initial Model 727-100 variant were Pratt & Whitney JT8D-7 or JT8D-9 turbofans, delivering 14,000 or 14,500 pounds of thrust, respectively. Each was equipped with a thrust-reverser to aid in slowing the aircraft on landing, thus enhancing its short field capability. Pratt & Whitney had designed the JT8D series engine especially for the 727, marking the first time in commercial aviation that a jet engine had been developed for a specific airplane.

The 727-100 had a wingspan of 108 feet and a wing area of 1,650 square feet. It was 133 feet 2 inches long and had a tail height of 34 feet. It weighed 170,000 pounds fully loaded and fueled, and had a service ceiling of 36,100 feet. Its cruising speed was 600 miles per hour, and it had a range in excess of 3,000 miles. Its passenger capacity was 131 persons, or less if a first class area was provided. Most important, it was capable of landing and taking off at airports where its larger sister could not operate.

To address this need, Boeing equipped the Model 727 with triple-slotted trailing edge flaps and new leading-edge slats to give the aircraft a low-speed landing and takeoff performance that would be necessary at smaller airports with runways shorter that 5,000 feet.

The leading edge of the wing has a slat on the outboard two-thirds of the span and Krueger flaps on the inboard portion of the wing. With these high-lift devices, a stalling speed of 121 miles per hour was obtained at the maximum landing weight of 160,000 pounds. The main landing gear employed two-wheel bogies instead of the four-wheel type used on the Model 707. To make it even more able to operate from remote locations, the 727 was also the first jetliner to carry its own built-in airstairs and auxiliary power unit for complete independence of ground support equipment.

Boeing also put the 727 airframe through unprecedented fatigue testing during the development process. Fatigue considerations were especially important because an aircraft specifically designed for shorter distances would obviously be making more cycles (each consisting of a takeoff and landing) in a given block of time than one designed for long-distance operations, and takeoffs and landings put more stress on an airframe than flying. The testing process was costly because it involved crushing entire airframes until they broke, but it demonstrated what was required to create an aircraft that could survive the stress of 20 years of service before the 727 reached its flight test phase. The process evolved as a standard part of aircraft development at Boeing. Ultimately, the Model 727 airframes would have more than 30, rather than merely 20, years of useful life. The durability of the 727 would be illustrated dramatically many years later. On April 2, 1982, a bomb placed by Libyan terrorists blew a hole nine feet across in a 727 en route to Athens, but the aircraft landed safely.

Although Boeing was able to launch the Model 727 program with substantial orders from United Air Lines and Eastern Airlines, additional sales were sluggish. A third airline joined the program on March 9, 1962, as TransWorld Airlines (TWA) placed its order for the first of an eventual 27 727-100 aircraft. On February 15, 1963, Ansett Australia and TransAustralian Airways ordered four and six 727-100s, respectively. While these were respectable sales, the numbers were still short of the 200 airframes that Boeing would

need to reach in order for the program to break even. With this in mind, the company sent a 727-100 on a 76,000-mile publicity tour of 26 countries that concluded in Seattle on November 3, 1963, just five days after United received its first 727-100 under a provisional FAA certificate.

On November 15, British West Indies Airways ordered three 727-100s and National Airlines placed an order for 13. In January 1964, two airlines in Japan announced orders. All Nippon Airways would take 8, and Japan Airlines would take 12. During February, both Eastern and United began regularly scheduled service with their 727-100s, and Northwest placed an order for 20 727-100s. South African Airways ordered six 727-100s on May 15, but it would be the only other new airline to order the aircraft during 1964.

The Model 727's nearest competitor, the similar British Aerospace Trident, had made its first flight a year ahead of the 727, but it would not enter service until two months after the 727. Soon, it was apparent that the operating costs for the 727 were below that of either the Caravelle or the Trident.

Originally delivered to Pan American in 1968 and dubbed *Clipper Golden Light*, this Boeing 727-121C was later transferred to Air Vietnam, and written off in 1974 at Phan Rang. The aircraft was en route from Da Nang to Saigon when a hijacker armed with two hand grenades demanded to be flown to Hanoi. It is not known why a landing was attempted at Phan Rang. The pilot aborted on final approach and the aircraft crashed as he attempted to go around for a second try.

Seen here coming in for a landing, this 727-030 was one of the Boeing 727-100 series aircraft originally sold to Germany's Lufthansa that later served with the United Parcel Service in the United States.

Meanwhile, on August 5, 1965, Boeing had formally announced the new 727-200, which would be 20 feet longer than the 727-100, permitting as many as 189 passengers in an all-tourist-class configuration. Its range was also extended to more than 3,500 miles when optimized for distance by maximum fuel and limited payload.

The 727-200 made its debut flight on July 27, 1967, and the first airline delivery, to Northeast Airlines, occurred on December 11. Northeast, which also operated the 727-100, put its first 727-200 into service three days later.

In 1991 the first Boeing 727-100 series aircraft delivered to United Air Lines in 1964 (a 727-022) was set aside to be preserved, in original United markings, at the Museum of Flight in Seattle.

A Boeing 727-235 in Pan American livery lifts off. Pan American used many of its 727s on its intra-European routes, including flights into West Berlin from locations in West Germany. As late as 1980, Pan American had domestic routes within Germany, but *not* within the continental United States. On the other hand, Germany's flag carrier, Lufthansa, could not legally operate into West Berlin for nearly half a century, but Pan American could.

During 1965, the program accelerated considerably, as Boeing announced new members of the 727 family. The 727-100C convertible freighter was introduced, offering an interior that could be reconfigured between all-cargo and all-passenger layouts by the customer. The cargo handling equipment installed in the 727-100C was adapted directly from that which had been used in the Boeing 707-320C. This option was especially attractive to smaller regional airlines around the world which needed the flexibility of an aircraft that could perform a variety of tasks.

A variation on the 727-100C that was marketed for a time under the designation 727-100Q was the "Quick Change" 727, which was easily and quickly convertible between an all-cargo configuration or a passenger configuration through the use of seats and galleys attached to removable pallets. The first delivery of the 727-100C variant, to Northwest Airlines, came on April 13, 1966. The first "Quick Change" 727-100QC went to United Air Lines a month later.

On the day after Christmas in 1967, Boeing reached the milestone of its 500th Model 727 delivery. In the four years since the type had gone into scheduled service, Boeing had sold more than double the number necessary for the program to break even. Boeing was emerging as the world's leading maker of jetliners. Indeed, the 727 was probably one of the factors that helped Boeing survive when it faced the most serious business crisis in its history.

With the cancellation of the Model 707 supersonic transport program and the loss of the C-5 U.S. Air Force airlifter program, the Boeing Company had almost disappeared. Layoffs had reached the point where people were saying, "the last person to leave Seattle should turn off the lights." Of course, both Boeing and Seattle weathered the storm, but it was touch and go for a time. Through it all, the robust sales of the Model 727 were a light in the dark that was never turned off. By September 1972, marked by an order from Delta Air Lines for 14 aircraft, a total of 1,000 727s had been sold.

In April 1971, with Lufthansa and Air Algerie leading the way, a new, modernized interior configuration was introduced. Although the basic interior dimensions remained the same, the redesign made the cabin appear more spacious, and its popularity with passengers led to its becoming standard.

In June 1972, Boeing delivered its first "Advanced" 727-200 to All Nippon Airways. This configuration, which logically might have been designated 727-300, would become the standard for subsequent 727-200 deliveries. There would never be a 727-300. The Advanced 727-200 had the same dimensions as the 727-200, but was distinguished by a gross weight of 191,000 pounds and a choice of engines that included the Pratt & Whitney JT8D-17R rated at 17,400 pounds of thrust. The gross weight of the 727-200 eventually was raised to 208,000 pounds, and three "heavyweights" delivered to Sterling Airways in Denmark had a gross weight of 210,000 pounds.

The range of the Advanced 727-200 was also impressive. In 1973 its capability was demonstrated by a 3,975-mile nonstop flight from Toronto to Copenhagen in Denmark. This clearly established the 727-200's versatility. The 727-200 was also the first jetliner capable of operating from extremely high-elevation airports, such as Bogota, Colombia (8,355 feet elevation), Cuzco, Peru (10,800 feet), and LaPaz, Bolivia (13,358 feet).

Perhaps the most dramatic operation ever conducted by a Boeing 727 was the famous "Last Flight from Da Nang." In the spring of 1975, the North Vietnamese army had launched the offensive that would culminate in the fall of South Vietnam on April 30. As North Vietnamese troops pushed south, massive streams of refugees fled south to escape.

As the North Vietnamese were closing in on Da Nang, South Vietnam's second largest city, World Airways of Oakland, California, was hired to make 20 evacuation flights from Da Nang under government charter. World Airways President Edward Daly brought two of his six 727-100Cs to Saigon personally to conduct the operation. However, after only three flights had been made, the U.S. Embassy canceled the contract due to the deteriorating situation.

Daly ignored official advice and, on March 29, he flew the two 727s to Da Nang in hopes of rescuing women and children. When the first plane landed, with Daly aboard, thousands of people rushed the plane and clambered aboard anywhere they could. Daly stood at the airstairs using the butt of a pistol to knock off the South Vietnamese soldiers who had clubbed women and children out of the way and were trying to climb aboard the already overloaded plane.

With the runway full of people racing toward the airplane, the flight's captain, Ken Healy, took off from a taxiway of about 5,000 feet in length that was parallel to the main runway. Despite being hit by a hand grenade, several bullets, and striking a pole on takeoff, the aircraft struggled into the air. Because it was determined that several people had climbed into the landing gear wells as the aircraft was taxiing, the gear could not be retracted without crushing them, so the aircraft had to fly with its gear up. With the extended gear creating tremendous aerodynamic drag, it took the aircraft more than two hours to make the usual 40 minute flight to Saigon.

When the aircraft landed, the crew estimated that they had carried approximately 338 people, roughly twice the normal passenger capacity of a 727-100. This number included approximately 60 in the cargo compartments and 8 in the gear wells. Daly was dismayed to find that only 11 women and children were among the people that he had rescued.

In December 1977, the Model 727, already the largest-selling commercial aircraft in history, became the first airliner type in history to carry more than a billion passengers. In 1978, as total orders for the Model 727 topped 1,500, Boeing announced the Model 757, a jetliner that was seen as the ultimate successor to the Model 727. It was planned that production of the trijet would end in 1984, as the Model 757 became available for service. On September 29, 1981, Boeing created the final 727 variant, the 727-200F, as a special order of 15 freighters for Federal Express.

The launch customers for the Model 727 were ultimately the two largest customers. United's 230 aircraft included 88 727-100s, 38 727-100Cs, and 104 727-200s. The 167 aircraft ordered by American Airlines included 58 727-100s and 109 727-200s.

Eastern Airlines was a close third with 163 aircraft, including 50 727-100s and 88 727-200s. In fourth place, Delta Air Lines acquired 116, all of them 727-200s. Fifth place Braniff ordered 97, including 6 727-100s, 18 727-100Cs, and 73 727-200s. TWA was a close sixth with 92, including 27 727-100s, 8 727-100Cs, and 57 727-200s. Rounding out the top seven was Northwest Airlines, with 85, including 20 727-100s, 12 727-100Cs, and 53 727-200s.

Pan American, which was the launch customer for Boeing's Stratocruiser, as well as the Model 707 and Model 747, bought only 35 Model 727 aircraft because

An in-flight image of a Boeing 727-227 in the markings of Braniff International Airways. Beginning in May 1965, Braniff bought 97 tri-jets from the Seattle planemaker. These included a half-dozen 727-127s, followed by 18 727-127Cs and 73 727-227s like the one pictured.

most of its route structure involved long-distance international flights better suited to larger aircraft.

Among airlines outside the United States, Lufthansa was the largest customer for the Model 727, with a total of 53. These included 16 727-100s, 11 727-100Cs, and 26 727-200s. Air Canada and Mexicana each acquired 39 aircraft, all of them 727-200s, except 4 727-100s sold to Mexicana. A close fourth among foreign airlines buying directly from Boeing was Spain's Iberia, with 37, all of them 727-200s. Japan's All Nippon was the leading operator in the Far East, with 35, of which 27 were 727-200s.

The order placed by Federal Express for 15 727-200Fs was the largest for that variant. Most of the 727 freighters that are flying in the twenty first century are aftermarket conversions of other Model 727 airframes that were originally delivered by Boeing as passenger aircraft or convertibles.

Other major airlines that bought Model 727 aircraft directly from the manufacturer were Aerolineas Argentinas (7), Air Algerie (11), Air Florida (5), Air France (29), Air Portugal (11), Alaska Airlines (10), Alitalia (18), Ansett of Australia (22), Germany's Condor (8), Continental Airlines (47), Canadian Pacific Airlines (CP Air) (6), Frontier Airlines (8), General American Transportation Corporation (GATX) (6), Hughes AirWest (13), Iranair (9), Iraqi Airways (6), Japan Airlines (12), Jugoslav Airlines (JAT) (11), LAN-Chile (5), Libyan Arab Airlines (11), National Airlines (38), Northeast Airlines

(19), Olympic Airways (6), Pacific Southwest Airlines (PSA) (37), Republic Airlines (7), Royal Air Maroc (8), Singapore Airlines (10), South African Airways (10), Sterling (8), Turk Hava Yollari (Turkish airlines) (10), Tunis Air (10), USAir (12), Viacao do Sao Paolo (6), Western Air Lines (46), World Airways (6), and Yemen Airways (5).

Commercial operators buying four or fewer Model 727s from Boeing included Air Charter International, Air Jamaica, Airlift International, American Capital Aviation, American Flyers, Ariana, Avianca, British West Indies Airways, China Airlines, Cruzeiro, Dominicana, Ethiopian Airlines, Executive Jet Aviation, Faucett, Hapag Lloyd, Icelandair, International Flight Research, International Lease Finance, Japan Domestic, Kuwait Airways, LAB of Bolivia, Lineas Aereas Centroamericanas Sociedad Anonima (LACSA) of Costa Rica, Nigeria Airways, Ozark Airlines, Pacific Airlines, Polynesian Airlines, Piedmont Airlines, Southern Air Transport, Syrian Arab Airlines, Tigerair, Transair of Sweden, Varig of Brazil, and WardAir of Canada. In addition to these customers, the International Telephone & Telegraph Company bought a single 727-100 for its own use. Many other operators would acquire secondhand 727s from airlines who bought them from Boeing.

Unlike the situation with the Model 707/717 family, Boeing had no direct sales for a military derivative of the Model 727. However, the governments of Cameroon, Jordan, and Nigeria each ordered one to use as an executive transport, as did the U.S. Federal Aviation Administration (FAA). The latter agency also acquired at least one former Lufthansa Model 727.

The three Model 727 aircraft that were in the inventory of the U.S. Air Force at the turn of the century and identified by the designation C-22 were all former airline aircraft. The C-22A was a former Lufthansa aircraft acquired from the FAA in 1984, and the three C-22Bs were former National Airlines 727s acquired from the airline in 1983. At the turn of the century, only the C-22Bs were in service, and all were assigned to the 201st Airlift Squadron of District of Columbia Air National Guard, where they were used as personnel transports.

The last delivery of a Model 727 in passenger configuration was made to USAir on April 6, 1984. This was followed in September by the last Model 727—a 727-200F—turned over to Federal Express.

Although production had ended, the service life of the Model 727 stretched out to the turn of the century and beyond, with the number of passengers topping the five billion mark. Indeed, nearly 1,500 727s were still flying at the turn of the century. Individual aircraft also achieved important milestones. The very first 727-100 delivered to United Air Lines was finally retired in January 1991 after nearly three decades of continuous service, making its last flight to Seattle and a permanent home at the Museum of Flight. During its career, the aircraft logged 94,492 hours and 48,057 cycles, and it had carried more than three million passengers. United estimated that the aircraft, which had originally cost $4.4 million, had earned $300 million in revenue.

Between November 1962 and September 1984, Boeing built 1,832 Model 727 aircraft, and sold all but the original prototype, which was scrapped after serving for many years as a company-owned test-bed aircraft. Of the 1,832, 408 were 727-100s, 164 were 727-100Cs, 1,245 were 727-200s, and the balance were 727-200Fs.

Of the other "T"-tailed small jetliners that were introduced in 1962–1963, the production totals for the British Aerospace Trident and the BAC-111 were 117 and 230, respectively, and neither of the Soviet aircraft attracted much interest outside of the Soviet Union and the airlines of its satellite nations.

Among all of the airliners—piston, turboprop, and jet—of the twentieth century, only Boeing's Model 737 was produced in greater numbers than the Model 727.

A 727-222 that was delivered to United Air Lines late in 1968 and scrapped in 1994. United's total order of 230 tri-jets stood for decades as the largest commercial acquisition of any single aircraft type by a single operator to be placed in Seattle. The total included 88 727-122s, 38 727-122, and 104 727-222 aircraft such as the one seen here.

CHAPTER TWELVE

THE DC-9:

Douglas Competes for the Short-Haul Market

By the late fifties, planemakers in Europe and America were racing to get the first generation of practical, long-range jetliners into service. Between October 1958 and September 1959, the de Havilland Comet 4, the Boeing 707, and the Douglas DC-8 all entered service.

As these aircraft came to life, the projects that eventually led to the Boeing 727, the Douglas DC-9, and de Havilland DH-121 (later British Aerospace Trident) were taking shape in the outer edges of these firms' respective engineering departments. While the lion's share of engineering resources were being allotted to such high-profile projects as the 707, DC-8, and Comet, respectively, efforts directed at developing smaller jets to serve smaller airports and lesser density routes proceeded at the proverbial snail's pace.

As Boeing entered the short-range jetliner market, so too did the Douglas Aircraft Company. However, just as Douglas had lagged behind its Seattle-based rival in the introduction of a large, longer-range jetliner, so too did it let Boeing take the lead with a smaller jet.

The Boeing 727 is often seen as the sixties jet-propelled equivalent of the ubiquitous Douglas DC-3 propliner of the thirties—*and* it would seem logical for Douglas to have produced the first such jet. However, for its day, the 24-passenger DC-3 was not a small airliner, and by the fifties, Douglas had clearly refocused its attention on the largest class of airliners. The DC-8 was a more natural extension of the DC-6/DC-7 lineage than something smaller.

Of course, as the big jetliners earned headlines—as well as their place in popular culture—even before their first flights, the airlines were asking for the *shorter-range* jets.

As has been pointed out above, the remarkable DC-3 had revolutionized air travel in the late thirties by bringing safe, reliable air transportation to many small and medium-size cities, and linking them to one another and to the outside world—in short, for making air travel available. Two decades later, the airlines were ready to make *jet* travel available as soon as the planemakers made the jets available to fly into the airports served by the DC-3.

Douglas considered many options in addition to designing a new aircraft from the ground up. One option was a shortened DC-8—as the Boeing 720 was an abbreviated 707—but this idea didn't fly with potential customers. The most serious alternative was licensing a short-

The Douglas DC-9 series prototype was the original DC-9-10 that made its first flight on February 25, 1965. The company would produce 142 DC-9-10 series aircraft under the specific designations DC-9-11 and DC-9-15.

The Douglas DC-9-30 first flew in 1966. The actual first aircraft went into service with Midway Airlines in 1967 as a DC-9-31 and was scrapped in 1993.

Seen at Los Angeles International Airport are two of the fleet of McDonnell Douglas DC-9-31s operated by Hughes AirWest. They were known in company advertising as "bananas" because of their shape and color.

would be smaller than the Boeing 727 and capable of landing on shorter runways than the Boeing trijet. Douglas was beating the Boeing 727 at its own game.

Eventually, Boeing would respond with the Model 737, which, in its initial configuration, was smaller yet. Ironically, as time went on, the Model 727, Model 737, and DC-9 would all evolve into larger and larger variants, with none of the follow-on versions of the three types being smaller than the initial ones.

The first flight of the DC-9-10 would occur on February 25, 1965, 24 months after that of the Boeing Model 727-100, but 26 months ahead of the Boeing Model 737-100. The latter was a more direct competitor, because the 737 and the DC-9 were

range jet that was already in production—specifically the French Sud-Aviation Caravelle, a twinjet that first flew in 1955 and that entered service in May 1959, a month before the DC-8. On February 10, 1960, Sud Aviation and Douglas formally agreed that the Long Beach planemaker would have the marketing rights in North America and elsewhere for the French jet, and that Douglas would also have the option to start manufacturing Caravelles in California. Indeed, over the ensuing months, a Caravelle in Douglas markings made the rounds of potential customers.

In December 1960, Boeing announced that it was building the Model 727 trijet. Douglas would continue to tout the Caravelle until the spring of 1963, although it never actually put it into production in the United States.

On April 8, 1963, Douglas finally and formally announced that the Caravelle was out, and a newer, smaller Douglas jet was in. To no one's surprise, this Douglas twinjet would be designated as the DC-9. It

about the same size, and both were a third smaller than the 727.

The size and short-field capability of the first-generation DC-9s proved to be popular with carriers operating regional routes where there would not be enough passengers to fill a Boeing 727. Beginning with the first one placed into service by Delta Air Lines on December 8, 1965, Douglas would deliver 142 DC-9-10 series aircraft under the subtype designations DC-9-11 and DC-9-15.

The engine choice of the entire DC-9 family would be Pratt & Whitney's JT8D family of turbofan engines, the same family developed originally for the Boeing 727 and subsequently used by Boeing for the initial variants of the 737 family.

Unlike the 727, which required a three-person flight crew, the cockpit of the DC-9 was designed for a two-member crew by eliminating the need for the flight engineer. Other features that would be common to all versions of the DC-9 were built-in boarding stairs for use where jetways are not available and passenger cabins designed for optimum passenger comfort and convenience. Economy class seating would be five abreast, which the manufacturer would point out as being consistently preferred in passenger surveys over the six-across seating in other single-aisle jetliners such as the DC-8 and the Boeing jetliners.

A "wide look" interior that would be introduced in 1973 was seen to provide a greater feeling of spaciousness by offering enclosed overhead racks for carry-on bags. The low ground clearance designed into the DC-9 family put the lower deck cargo bays at waist height, to allow loading and unloading without extensive specialized equipment.

The DC-9-10 prototype and the initial DC-9-11 production models each had a wingspan of 89 feet 4 inches and a length of 104 feet 4 inches, almost 30 feet shorter than the Boeing 727-100. They had a tail height of 27 feet 6 inches. They weighed 35,608 pounds fully loaded and fueled, and accommodated up to 90 passengers, depending on configuration, and had 600 cubic feet of cargo space on the lower deck. They were powered by a version of the Pratt & Whitney JT8D turbofan engine, in this case, the JT8D-5 or JT8D-7, with takeoff thrust ratings of 12,250 to 14,000 pounds, respectively.

In the decade after World War II, Douglas had the experience of seeing the DC-4 evolve into the larger DC-6 and DC-7. The idea was that a newer, larger aircraft need not be an entirely new aircraft. Adapting aspects of a smaller aircraft that would work just as well in a larger aircraft saved both money and development time. From this came the Douglas "Design for Growth" concept, by which the groundwork for an enlarged version of an aircraft was laid during the design process of the original prototype. For example, the flight deck and the fuselage diameter and cross-section would remain the same under the Design for Growth concept, even as subsequent DC-9 variants became longer.

The DC-8 had been designed so that it could be enlarged, although that capacity was not exercised until the development of the "Super Sixty" series late in the 1960s. With the DC-9, however, the Design for Growth concept was implemented on a grander scale and much more quickly.

The DC-8s were "stretched" as the program evolved, but with the DC-9, a road map for subtypes of varying lengths was part of the plan from the

beginning, and it would continue to unfold for four decades. The DC-8-10 through DC-8-40 were all the same size, but every successive subvariant of the DC-9 would be larger. From the DC-9-20 to the DC-9-80, the fuselage lengths would step up 15, 6, 8, and 14 feet, so that the DC-9-80 series would be more than 43 feet—or half again—longer than the original DC-9s.

While the fuselage lengths would increase, a common high-lift wing was developed for use in all the variants from the DC-9-20 series through the DC-9-50 series. Designed with a system of leading edge slats for improved short-field performance, this wing had a span of 93 feet 4 inches—4 feet greater than that of the DC-9-10—and an area of 1,000.7 square feet.

Because they were all part of an overall master plan, the members of the DC-9 "family" would be designated in order of size rather than chronology. The DC-9-20 series was so designated because it was larger than the DC-9-10 and smaller than the DC-9-30, even though it was actually introduced between the DC-9-40 and the DC-9-50.

The second DC-9 would be the DC-9-30, which first flew on August 1, 1966. The DC-9-30 was 119 feet 3 inches long and had a tail height of 27 feet 6 inches.

The McDonnell Douglas DC-9-40 first flew in 1968, and the actual first aircraft went into service with Northwest Airlines later in the year as a DC-9-41.

The executive interior of a McDonnell Douglas DC-9-30 series aircraft operated by the Italian air force. Why the Italian military would need such accommodations can only be imagined.

The McDonnell Douglas DC-9-50 first flew in 1974, and the actual first aircraft went into service with Hawaiian Airlines the following year as a DC-9-51.

Nearly 15 feet longer than its predecessor, it accommodated up to 115 passengers and had 895 cubic feet of cargo space beneath the floor of the main cabin. Most of the DC-9-30s would be powered by either Pratt & Whitney JT8D-7 or JT8D-9 engines delivering 14,000 or 14,500 pounds of thrust, respectively. Others were equipped with the JT8D-11 or the JT8D-15, with 15,000 or 15,500 pounds of thrust, respectively. Having first entered service with Eastern Airlines on February 1, 1967, the DC-9-30 went on to become the most widely used member of the DC-9 family, accounting for approximately 60 percent of the entire fleet.

In addition to 570 commercial DC-9-30s delivered to the airlines, 43 were delivered to the U.S. military services under the conveniently coincidental designation C-9. Acquired in 1967 for use as aeromedical transports, or ambulance planes, there were 21 DC-9-30s delivered to the Air Force as the C-9A Nightingale between August 10, 1968, and February 1973, and 19 to the U.S. Navy and Marine Corps as the C-9B Skytrain II between May 8, 1973, and mid-1976. The original "Skytrain" appellation had been assigned four decades earlier to the military version of the Douglas DC-3, which flew with the USAAF and U.S. Air Force under the designations C-47 and C-53, and with the U.S. Navy and Marine Corps under the designation R4D.

An additional three DC-9-30s were delivered to the U.S. Air Force in 1975 as executive transports under the designation VC-9C, and two went to the Kuwait Air Force in the aeromedical transport configuration.

The C-9A and C-9B were specifically designed for the movement of stretcher and ambulatory patients, with the latter accommodated in aft-facing commercial airline-type seats. They can airlift 40 stretcher patients or 40 ambulatory plus four stretcher patients—or various combinations. A hydraulically operated folding ramp allows efficient loading and unloading of stretcher patients and special medical equipment.

In addition, these aircraft each have a special care area with a separate ventilation system for patients requiring isolation or intensive care; 11 vacuum and therapeutic oxygen outlets positioned in sidewall service panels at stretcher tier locations; a 28-VDC outlet in the special care area; a medical refrigerator for preserving whole blood and biological drugs; a medical supply work area with sink, medicine storage section, and work table; and fore-and-aft galleys and lavatories. Twenty-two 115-VAC/60-hertz electrical outlets located throughout the cabin permit the use of cardiac monitors, respirators, incubators, and infusion pumps at any location within the cabin. There is also a station for a medical crew director that includes a desk, communication panel, and a control panel to monitor cabin temperature, therapeutic oxygen, and vacuum system. An auxiliary power unit provides electrical power for uninterrupted cabin air conditioning, quick servicing during stops, and self-starting for the twin-jet engines.

At the turn of the century, the C-9 fleet was still quite active, with the U.S. Air Force C-9A Nightingales operated for the Air Mobility Command by the 375th

Airlift Wing at Scott Air Force Base, Illinois. They were assigned to the 374th Airlift Wing in Japan for use in the Pacific theater and to the 435th Airlift Wing in Germany for use in the European and Middle East theaters of operation.

The DC-9-30 would also have the distinction of being, perhaps, the last "Douglas" aircraft. When the type made its first flight in 1966, the Douglas Aircraft Company was in the final throes of the financial crisis that forced it to find a merger partner to ensure survival. The merger of Douglas with the McDonnell Aircraft Company of St. Louis was agreed upon on January 13, 1967. When the first DC-9-30 was delivered two weeks later, it was unofficially a McDonnell Douglas aircraft. On April 28, the merger became official, and the McDonnell Douglas Corporation became a reality. All the succeeding DC-9s would be "McDonnell Douglas," rather than "Douglas," aircraft.

The Long Beach factory continued to be called the "Douglas" component of the combined corporation, but the sign atop the former Douglas building at Long Beach now read "McDonnell Douglas." However, the neon sign on the final assembly hanger, still

clearly visible to the millions who drive the San Diego Freeway every week, says "Fly DC Jets."

The third member of this "DC Jet" family was the DC-9-40, which first flew on November 28, 1967, and was first delivered on February 29, 1968, to the Scandinavian Airlines System (SAS). The DC-9-40 was 125 feet 6 inches long and had a tail height of 28 feet, 6 inches greater than its predecessors. Seating was available for up to 125 passengers, 10 more than the popular DC-9-30s. Below-floor cargo space totaled 1,019 cubic feet. The choice of available engines included the Pratt & Whitney JT8D-9, JT8D-11, and JT8D-15, delivering 14,500, 15,000, and 15,500 pounds of thrust, respectively.

Introduced fourth, the DC-9-20 series (technically, all were DC-9-21 aircraft) was developed specifically for SAS routes to the small airports in northern Norway and Sweden. It was the same length as the DC-9-10 series, but, with its larger wing and more powerful engine, it was optimized for operation from these very short runways. It combined the fuselage of the DC-9-10 series with a high-lift wing developed for the DC-9-30 series. Power was provided by two

A McDonnell Douglas DC-9-51 sold to Ghana Airways in 1978. Formed in 1958 with the help of British Overseas Airways, the carrier became entirely state owned three years later. After an ill-fated flirtation with Soviet-made equipment, which was politically fashionable in Africa during the 1960s, Ghana settled down with British and American aircraft.

The prototype of the McDonnell Douglas DC-9-80 Super Eighty series, circa 1979. It was retained as a company demonstrator.

JT8D-9s with 14,500 pounds thrust each, or 15,000-pound JT8D-11s. The DC-9-21 first flew on September 18, 1968, the ninth anniversary of the entry into service of its older sister, the DC-8. The first delivery of a DC-9-21 to SAS occurred on December 11, less than two months after its first flight. Only ten DC-9-20s would be built.

While new DC-9 variants debuted annually between 1965 and 1968, McDonnell Douglas focused the attention of the Long Beach facility on the DC-10 jumbo jet, which would make its first flight on August 29, 1970, and enter service a year later. This enormous project involved an all-new aircraft that was larger than anything the company had ever done, and a great deal of engineering and production resources had to be devoted to it. Thus, the DC-9 family would not be enlarged until the huge DC-10 was introduced and firmly established in the marketplace.

The DC-9-50 made its first flight on December 17, 1974, the 71st anniversary of the Wright brothers' first flight at Kitty Hawk, and the 39th anniversary of the first flight of the great Douglas DC-3. Six years had passed since the previous debut of a DC-9 variant, and more than two years had passed since the first flight of the fourth and last commercial variant of the big DC-10.

The DC-9-50 was 133 feet 6 inches long, making it the first DC-9 variant to match the length of the Boeing 727-100. With five more rows of seats than the popular DC-9-30, maximum passenger capacity was 139. The engines would be either the Pratt & Whitney JT8D-15 or JT8D-17, which delivered 15,500 or 16,000 pounds of thrust, respectively. The first airline delivery took place on August 15, 1975.

There would be no DC-9-60 nor DC-9-70. The DC-9-70 would have been powered by the General

The first McDonnell Douglas Super Eighty delivered to American Airlines was a DC-9-82 (MD-82) that was turned over to the carrier during the summer of 1983. The aircraft now had the "MD" designator, but the big neon sign at the Long Beach factory still read "Fly DC Jets."

Electric/SNECMA (Société National d'Etudes et Construction de Moteurs d'Avion) CFM56 series high-bypass turbofan engines used on the DC-8-70 re-engining project, but the DC-9-70 project was cancelled in favor of moving on to the DC-9-80 program with an advanced Pratt & Whitney engine.

The DC-9-80 series would be the final DC-9 variant. Better known in its early days as the "Super Eighty," it would eventually be redesignated as the MD-80 series. The catalyst for the Super Eighty was a growing demand for a still-larger DC-9 from the major operators of the DC-9-50, including Eastern Airlines, Republic Airlines, and Swissair—all of whom promised significant orders if McDonnell Douglas would build the aircraft. Swissair would make good on its promise, but Eastern was headed for financial trouble that ultimately led to bankruptcy in 1991, and Republic would be absorbed into Northwest Airlines in 1987 after buying just a handful of the promised aircraft.

The DC-9-80 was first flown on October 18, 1979, five years after its predecessor. For its debut, it was crewed by veteran test pilot H.H. "Knick" Knickerbocker, John Lane, and Virginia Clare, who had the distinction of being the first woman flight test engineer to make the first flight of a new model McDonnell Douglas aircraft. Knickerbocker, project test pilot during the certification phase for the MD-80, said the plane "flew really well from the start. It was an honest plane, you could count on it."

The Super Eighty was 147 feet 10 inches long—more than 14 feet longer than the DC-9-50—and it had a tail height of 29 feet, 5 inches. The Super Eighty's wingspan was 107 feet 10 inches and the wing's area was 1,279 square feet. The new wing was like the wing used on the four previous DC-9 variants, with leading edge slats for improved short-field performance, but it was scaled up nearly 30 percent in size. The gross takeoff weight for the prototype would be 140,000 pounds, which was increased to 142,000 pounds for the initial DC-9-81 (later MD-81) production series.

The powerplant used for the prototype and the early aircraft of the DC-9-81 production series would be the Pratt & Whitney JT8D-209, rated at 18,500 pounds of takeoff thrust. The Pratt & Whitney JT8D-200 series engines were based on the earlier JT8D series and had been developed under NASA sponsorship. The new engines used improved technology, including a new six-stage low-pressure compressor and a new bypass duct, to provide more power while

being quieter and more fuel efficient. Meanwhile, the new engine had a diameter of 56 inches, just 14 inches greater than that of the earlier JT8Ds, and still 200 inches smaller than the diameter of the CFM56 engines being used by the rival Boeing 737 family.

Subsequent Super Eighty series aircraft included the DC-9-82, the DC-9-83, the DC-9-87, and the DC-9-88. All of these would have the same wingspan as the DC-9-81. The DC-9-82 and DC-9-83 would be the same length as the DC-9-81, but the DC-9-87, which was conceived as a DC-9-30 replacement, had a fuselage that was 119 feet 1 inch long, 2 inches shorter than the DC-9-30, and the DC-9-88 was 130 feet 4 inches long. The respective certified gross takeoff weights of these four aircraft would be 149,500 pounds, 160,000 pounds, 149,500 pounds, and 140,000 pounds.

A variety of Pratt & Whitney JT8D-200 series engines were certified for use on the Super Eighty family. In addition to the JT8D-209, a customer might choose the JT8D-217 with 20,000 pounds of thrust, the JT8D-217A/C with 20,000 pounds of thrust, or the JT8D-219 with 21,000 pounds of thrust.

The first DC-9-81 entered service with Swissair on October 5, 1980, and the first operations within the United States were by Pacific Southwest Airlines

A McDonnell Douglas DC-9-81 (MD-81) in Swissair livery. The Swiss carrier was a major Super Eighty customer.

A McDonnell Douglas DC-9-81 (MD-81) originally delivered to Hawaiian Air in 1981, but later operated by Continental Airlines.

A McDonnell Douglas DC-9-82 (MD-82) delivered to TWA in 1983. The carrier would eventually acquire a fleet of more than 20 factory-fresh Super Eighty ships.

(PSA) two months later on December 17. The first DC-9-82 entered service with Republic Airlines in August 1981; the first DC-9-83 entered service with Finnair under the MD-83 designation in July 1985; the first DC-9-87 entered service with both Austrian Airlines and Finnair under the MD-87 designation in November 1987; and the first DC-9-88 entered service with Delta Air Lines under the MD-88 designation in January 1988.

The decision by the McDonnell Douglas Corporation to reinvent the Super Eighty family with the "MD" prefix had evolved as the first production models were rolling off the assembly line and as the new line was being marketed. The idea was based on a number of factors that were more from a marketing than technical point of view, because the DC-9-80 was, technically speaking, a DC 9 and not a new aircraft. In fact, it was originally certified through an amendment of the DC-9 certificate, and the DC-9-80s were built on the same Long Beach assembly line as the aircraft from DC-9-10 to DC-9-50, using the same equipment and tooling.

The primary, and most obvious, reason for the change was that the McDonnell Douglas Corporation wanted to assert the corporate identity, retire the old "DC" (for "Douglas Commercial") prefix, and give this new generation of jetliners a "McDonnell Douglas" appellation. Indeed, the stretched DC-10 would become the "MD-11" rather than the "DC-11."

A secondary reason for the new MD-80 nomenclature was to create the impression of a new aircraft. The airframe was clearly that of a DC-9, but it was powered by a new generation of engines, and the digital avionics in the familiar flight deck represented a quantum leap from the "round dial" environment of the original DC-9 variants.

In December 1982, McDonnell Douglas Corporation officially terminated the DC-9 program. All of the 108 DC-9-81s and DC-9-82s that had been built and/or delivered since 1980 were retroactively redesignated as MD-81s and MD-82s. From January 1983, all new aircraft carried the "MD" prefix.

Actually, the DC-9 program had ended in October 1982 with the delivery of the last DC-9-50 series aircraft. Over the course of 18 years, 976 of the twin jets had been built. This total included 142 DC-9-10s; 10 DC-9-20s; 570 DC-9-30s; 69 DC-9-40s; 77 DC-9-50s; and 108 Super Eighties delivered under the DC-9-80 series designations. The military C-9s were included among the 570 DC-9-30 airframes. This made the DC-9 the biggest selling commercial aircraft in Douglas history. It even outsold the commercial version of the DC-3.

The program's largest customer through the DC-9-50 series was Eastern Airlines, which began with an order for 15 DC-9-14s and subsequently bought 72 DC-9-31s and 5 DC-9-51s. The second largest customer was Delta Air Lines, which acquired 14 DC-9-14s and 63 DC-9-32s.

TransWorld Airlines (TWA) was another important domestic customer in the early days of the program, with 13 DC-9-10 series aircraft, but it did not buy additional, later variants until the DC-9-82, of which it would take 18. A major domestic carrier that was *not* a customer in the early days, but which emerged as the most important single Super Eighty customer was American Airlines, which would acquire more than 165 DC-9-82s and DC-9-83s.

The McDonnell Douglas flight line at Long Beach, California, mid-1980s, showing a line of DC-9-80 (MD-80) aircraft being prepped for final delivery. The Super Eighty series provided the company with a renaissance of sorts after several years of dwindling sales.

The DC-9 was immediately popular with American regional carriers, notably with Allegheny Airlines, which became USAir in 1979. As Allegheny, the airline bought 39 DC-9-31s and 7 DC-9-51s. As USAir, the company took 17 and 3, respectively. In 1987, USAir acquired Pacific Southwest Airlines (PSA), which then owned a small number of early series DC-9s and which had bought 28 Super Eighties from McDonnell Douglas.

Another important regional airline was Republic Airlines, which was formed in 1979 through a merger of North Central and Southern Airlines. North Central came to the merger with 20 DC-9-31s and 18 DC-9-51s, while Southern contributed a total of 11 DC-9s of various types. Before it was, in turn, absorbed into Northwest Airlines in 1987, Republic itself bought 6 DC-9-51s and 8 DC-9-82s.

Other notable domestic customers for the DC-9-10 through DC-9-50 series included Bonanza Air, Continental Airlines, Hawaiian Airlines, Hughes Air West, Northeast Airlines, Ozark Airlines, Texas International Airlines, and West Coast Airlines. In addition to American Airlines, other carriers that became important to the Super Eighty program—that had not previously been involved as customers—included Air Cal (Air California), Muse Air, and New York Air.

Scandinavian Airlines System (SAS) was the biggest foreign customer for the early series DC-9s, beginning with five DC-9-32s and a pair of DC-9-33F

freighters. As noted above, the DC-9-20 series was created specifically for SAS, and it acquired all 10 DC-9-21s. The airline went on to buy an additional 36 DC-9-41s, 10 DC-9-81s, and 8 DC-9-82s. Italy's Alitalia bought 36 DC-9-32s and added 21 DC-9-82s. Swissair acquired 5 DC-9-15s, 15 DC-9-32s, 12 DC-9-51s, and, later, 23 DC-9-81s. Swissair's keen interest in the potential of the Super Eighty series had been one of the reasons that McDonnell Douglas had decided to undertake the ambitious project.

Among the other notable foreign carriers who purchased the DC-9-10 through DC-9-50 series were Aeromexico, Air Jamaica, Air Canada, Ansett of Australia, Austrian Airlines, Avensa, British West Indies Airways, Caribair, East African Airways, Finnair, Garuda of Indonesia, Ghana Airways, Inex Adria, Jugoslovenski Aerotransport (JAT), Koninklijke Luchtvaart Maatschappij (KLM, Royal Dutch Airlines), Korean Air Lines, Martinair of the Netherlands, Saudia, Spain's Iberia, Spain's Aviaco, Sudflug, Trans-Australia Airways, Turk Hava Yollari (Turkish airlines), and Venezuela's Linea Aerea Venezolana (LAV).

While the purpose of this section is to focus on the DC-9-10 through DC-9-50 series, rather than the Super Eighty and MD-80 that evolved from it, we have chosen to round out the story with a sketch of the later evolution of the airframe that originally was designated as the DC-9.

One of the 18 McDonnell Douglas DC-9-82 (MD-82) aircraft delivered to TWA during the 1980s. The carrier would eventually acquire more than 100 Super Eighty aircraft.

During the 1980s, the number of MD-80s produced had surpassed the production total of DC-9s—even including those that had been delivered as MD-9-80s. By the end of the decade, the unfilled commercial backlog at the McDonnell Douglas Long Beach facility was at an all-time high—including firm orders for over 400 MD-80s—and the company was delivering record numbers of jetliners. The largest airline fleet of any single type of aircraft in the world was the American Airlines fleet of McDonnell Douglas MD-80s. In August 1989, American had accepted its 165th MD-80 and signed a purchase agreement that included another 100 MD-80 options. In June 1992, American took delivery

of the 1,024th MD-80, which was the milestone 2,000th twin-jet in the DC-9/MD-80 lineage.

In November 1989, McDonnell Douglas announced another DC-9 derivative that would complement the MD-80 on the Long Beach assembly line. Designated as MD-90, it first flew on February 22, 1993, powered by two International Aero Engines V2500 turbofans. After FAA certification in late 1994, the first delivery was made to launch customer Delta Air Lines in February 1995, and the aircraft entered revenue service in April 1995. The MD-90 was designed to be technically and economically competitive by incorporating many then-new cost-effective technologies, including new electrical and auxiliary power systems, an upgraded digital environmental control system, lightweight carbon brakes with a digital antiskid system, and significant improvements to the aircraft hydraulic system.

The MD-90 had the same wingspan as the MD-80, but it was almost five feet longer, at 152 feet 6 inches, and it accommodated up to 155 passengers, five-abreast in a typical mixed-class configuration. It had a range of up to 2,765 miles, slightly greater than of the MD-80. The International Aero Engines V2525-D5 turbofans of the production models delivered 25,000 pounds of thrust. The MD-90-30 production version had a maximum takeoff gross weight of 156,000

The McDonnell Douglas MD-90-30 prototype during a May 1994 test flight. The first flight of the MD-90 series occurred on February 22, 1993.

In March 1987, Delta Air Lines became the launch customer for the MD-88 series. Through the early 1990s, 120 of these aircraft would be delivered to Delta at Long Beach.

pounds, and the MD-90-30ER (Extended Range) increased the maximum gross weight to 166,000 pounds, providing a range increase to 2,750 miles with the addition of a 565-gallon auxiliary fuel tank.

In 1991, McDonnell Douglas announced plans for the MD-95, which would be the successor to the MD-87 as a replacement for the venerable DC-9-30. It would be 122 feet 6 inches long, making it about a yard longer than the DC-9-30 and the MD-87. The production version would be 124 feet long. While the MD-80 and MD-90 both had the longest wingspan of the overall series, the MD-95 had the same wingspan as the DC-9-20 through DC-9-50—93 feet 4 inches—with a wing area of 1,000.7 square feet.

In December 1996, just 14 months after the McDonnell Douglas MD-95 was introduced, the McDonnell Douglas Corporation was acquired by the Boeing Company. More than three decades after Douglas launched the DC-9 program, the direct descendant of that program was owned by the company that had been Douglas' biggest rival in 1965. A program begun before the McDonnell Douglas merger had outlived the McDonnell Douglas Corporation.

In a final irony, Boeing would adopt the MD-95 by renaming it with one of its own designations in the legendary 700 series. Boeing considered it too strong a step to give the next number in the sequence— "787"—to a small aircraft based on an older, non-Boeing design, so the company's designators got creative. Boeing reached back to the only "7-7" model number that had not been used by a *commercial* aircraft—"717." This number had been the original company model number for the military KC-135 series, and it was now *reused* for the MD-95. It was the only Boeing model number assigned twice to two aircraft that were actually put into production.

The new Boeing 717 flew for the first time on September 2, 1998, powered by a pair of advanced BMW/Rolls-Royce BR715 high-bypass turbofan engines rated at between 18,500 and 21,000 pounds of takeoff thrust, with lower fuel consumption, reduced exhaust emissions, and significantly lower noise levels than the powerplants on comparable airplanes. The first production 717-200 was delivered a year later on September 23, 1999, to AirTran Airways, the Orlando, Florida-based launch customer. By this time, TransWorld Airlines (TWA) had announced that it had chosen the 717 series to replace its existing DC-9 fleet.

The stated intention of the 717-200 could have been taken directly from the mission statement of the DC-9 at the time of its introduction more than a generation before. Boeing's marketing staff wrote that the 717-200 had been "designed specifically for efficient short-hop service, short-field operations, fast turnaround at airport gates, and the ability to sustain 8 to 12 one-hour flights every day, day after day. The 717-200 can easily serve the routes in this market, which average 300 miles or less. . . . In addition, the 717's exceptionally low trip cost allows operators to explore new markets with lower risk."

By the time of the first deliveries to AirTran Airways, 18 airlines in the United States, Europe, Asia, and the Middle East had signed on to receive the 100-passenger jetliner.

The program had come full circle, and after 35 years, the DC-9/MD-80/MD-90/717 lineage was firmly established as the second most successful (after the Boeing 737) airliner program in history. It is a powerful testament to the aircraft designers of the 1960s that after the passage of so much time, the same basic airframe designs were not only still in service, but they were still in production and selling briskly.

INDEX